THE PHILOSOPHY OF JESUS: REAL LOVE

by

Rev. Jules A. Delanghe

DORRANCE & COMPANY

Philadelphia

ADDRESSEES

This book is addressed to all "men of good will" and especially to the youth of today, searching desperately for the true meaning of life and of love. Hopefully it will also provide the reader with the key to the understanding of the Gospel.

Hard as it is to give a theoretical picture of the meaning of love, the practical application of this great principle is ever so much harder. The success of the practice of selfless love depends on one's sincerity and one's personal application. It also is a lifetime business. Yet without a sense of direction, traveling easily becomes an aimless wandering. This is the reason why I have tried to draw up a road-map based on the actual features of love's terrain and on the logic of the world's greatest expert in love-affairs. That the humble searcher for the true meaning of love may not find this work to be an impractical speculation is my fervent hope.

To all my friends who stood by me in the difficult task of analyzing the real meaning of love, I express my abiding gratitude.

CONTENTS

INTRODUCTION

Philosophy, as the word etymologically implies, is the love or natural attraction that people have for wisdom or for the ultimate constituents of everything that is real. We become wise when we know more about the nature and ultimate purpose of that which is real, when we can distinguish reality from fantasy and when we can put all real things in their right perspective.

The natural scientist gets his knowledge directly from sensory experience or laboratory tests. The philosopher arrives at his contact with reality from the reflection on the ultimate nature of things. Even though the natural scientist examines his objects from a physically closer point of view, still he knows less about their real nature, their origin and their ties to other forms of reality. In short his picture of reality is one-sided and incomplete. Unless he keeps in contact with the principles of philosophy which are certain, he is like an eye specialist who knows only the function of the eyes or like the legalist who is unable to discern the intent of the law. The philosopher who is sufficiently removed from the tree, so to speak, to be able to see the purpose of the forest, usually knows enough about trees not to attribute to them qualities which they do not possess. We say that the philosopher is "usually" aware of the obvious facts of nature. Some philosophers have been known to deny the well-known truth, such as denying the existence of man's free will, though limited it be. Non-factual speculation is what has given philosophy a bad name in the field of science.

The philosopher's contact with reality comes from general principles which he has learned through the experience of everyday living. Everybody knows from personal experience that "the whole is greater than its part." Similarly, through experience we automatically look for an adequate cause to account for the presence of a phenomenon or particular effect. All these so-called

1

inborn principles of common sense from which the philosopher logically deduces his conclusions are knowledge which he has gained through sense-observation. Conclusions which are contradicted by the facts of life or by the discoveries of natural sciences are therefore unjustifiable speculations. The fact that a good deal of philosophers have reached unwarranted conclusions does not mean that all philosophers were unrealistic in their manner of thinking. In the same way, the fact that empiricists and rationalists dispute over the nature of knowledge, the criterion of truth and the source of perception does not mean that their opinions are hopelessly irreconcilable. By qualifying the statement that "all knowledge comes to us through the senses" with the words *directly* or *indirectly*, we have removed the conflict which exists in this dispute.

Philosophy does not have all the right answers on the ultimate nature of everything that exists. In the same way the positive sciences still ignore the answer to the majority of their problems. Yet there is enough of well-balanced philosophy to give every person honestly looking for the truth a firm grip on life and a sound solution to his major difficulties. Our capacity of being able to find the truth is not crippled, provided that we do not let our senses blind our thinking and our selfishness destroy our values. Philosophy can improve its vision and that of other sciences just as non-philosophical disciplines can limit philosophy's unjustifiable speculations. Both sides can be of service to each other provided that they both are open to the combination of reason and of facts.

Of the many areas where philosophy has contributed to a better understanding of the universe, the contributions which it has made in the field of ethics are by far the most significant. In his search for the truth in everything he says and does, the honest philosopher has not only found the correct picture of reality but he has also found the real goodness and beauty of human behavior. Everyone who wants to be true to himself and sincere to others has the makings of a good philosopher. As far back as Zoroaster (660 B.C.-583 B.C.), the great prophet of Iran, we find evidence of great minds who tried to spell out the logic of human behavior or the true form of our approach to religion. Professing ethical dualism, Zoroaster declared

2

Ahura Mazda or Ormazd to be the Lord of Wisdom and the creator of the universe. Ahriman or Druj was said to be the devil or the spirit of evil. The prophet furthermore held that man as a free agent would eventually overcome the powers of evil and receive the reward of a resurrected life.

Some of the greatest minds on ethical thinking were doubtlessly the Greek philosophers of pre-Christian times. Even to this day the greatest part of Western civilization and of Christian philosophy is founded on the insights of Plato (c. 427-347 B.C.) and Aristotle (c. 384-322 B.C.). Plato maintained that the soul was immortal and that the health of the soul was more important than the health of the body. Man looks after the health of his soul by the practice of virtue just as he lets his spiritual health deteriorate by yielding to vice. In Plato's opinion, vice is worse than death and it is better to suffer injustice than to be the cause of unjust doings. To these conditions of human nature which determine our rational conduct, Aristotle added another element of capital importance, namely that of our natural sociability.*

While listening to these views, one cannot help noticing a striking resemblance with the philosophy of Jesus. "The eye," says Christ, "is the lamp of the body." So if we use our eyes for observing reality or if we look for the truth which is the same thing, then our "whole body will be full of light." Besides, you cannot try to find the correct picture of reality and at the same time distort this picture to suit yourself. "No one can serve two masters . . . God and Mammon." God stands for social justice or righteousness while Mammon stands for caring for one's self exclusively. We are advised to seek God's kingdom first, because the health of the soul comes before the health of the body. (Mt. 6, 22-33.) The same thought comes back in form of a question. "For what does it profit a man if he gains the whole world but suffer the loss of his soul?" (Mt. 16, 26.) According to Plato the health of the soul is achieved by the practice of virtue. According to Jesus the health of the mind is obtained by the search

* *Collier's Encyclopedia*, S.V. Plato.

3

for the truth. So important is it for us to stand up for the truth and suffer for its cause, that we should not be afraid of the harm which people may do to us, even if they go as far as to deprive us of our life. Such harm is only for a while. On the contrary we should be afraid of the punishment of God which is everlasting. (Mt. 10, 28.) In making this statement Christ was doubtlessly thinking about the short existence of our body in its present condition and of the permanent existence of our body in a transformed state.

What now is this health of the soul which, in Plato's words, is of greater value than the health of the body? What is this search for the truth which, in Christ's words, is worth more than one's life or one's family? Aristotle tells us in vague terms that it consists in living socially. Christ tells us in plain language that it consists in the observance of the Golden Rule. This precious gem of truth, this singular pearl of wisdom which can merit for us the eternal rewards of a glorious resurrection, is none other than the love of our neighbor. Christ does not suggest that we place society or the state above our family or even above our personal needs. He does not imply that lay people give up their right to personal property, although he wants his leaders to be more completely detached. He does, however, want all people to share their goods with the needy and to consider their belongings as though they were only entrusted to their care. In Christ's mind, communism and socialism just like compulsive celibacy are an attack on the individual's right to self-determination. Community property and celibate living do not serve their purpose unless the individual is free to withdraw at any given time.

The Golden Rule would not be so hard to follow if all people had at least a little bit of gratitude. Besides being good to the deserving, we are told to forgive our malefactors and treat them even with respect. Christ goes so far as to ask us to pray for those who intend to hurt us some more. All this is easier said than done. The philosopher may be able to make people see what is rational, but he cannot make people accept evangelic idealism on the basis of logic alone. Unless he himself gives evidence of unselfish dedication to his followers, his words of wisdom will have no response.

4

The role of philosophy is to teach good ethics. The role of religion is to carry them out. Philosophy makes an appeal to the mind only. Religion makes an appeal to the heart as well. Philosophy remains in the field of theory. Religion extends into the field of practice. The one solves the problems in general. The other solves the problems in a particular case. The first is cold and abstract; the second is warm and personal.

The whole purpose of religion and even of the Bible is to teach morality or rational human behavior. Purely speculative or dogmatic beliefs which have no bearing on morality are a total waste of time. Impractical theories are as worthless in religion as in any other rational discipline. Such improbable speculations can neither be backed up by Scripture or proven by logic. Rather than becloud our thinking, Christ aimed at enlightening our mind. If you examine the mysteries of Christianity closely, you will find that they are the result of taking literally certain passages of Scripture, where the writer's moral lesson is expressed in a figure of speech. No wholesome religion talks about mysteries except those which are apt to improve our conduct and whose existence is the result of logical deduction. Such mysteries are not mysterious as to their existence but only as to our personal inexperience of anything that is not material. From the principle of causality which we apply in everyday life we logically deduct the existence of an ultimate cause. Like all intelligent beings, the supreme being is also held to the application of reward.

Philosophy accepts God as an abstract principle. Religion accepts God as a concrete reality. The one is no good without the other. Religion without reason is only a form of superstition. Reason without religion is only a stream of words. The philosopher is like a lame man with good eyes. The religious-minded is like a blind man with good legs. If the blind man carries the lame man on his back, both men will reach the object of their journey. The synthesis of Christ's philosophy is to direct all our affection towards the real needs of humanity in a well-balanced fashion. Religion is the thing that helps the philosopher stick to his principles, whether by faith in a future reward or by someone's heroic example of unselfish dedication. Without religion, reason is like a grain which fails to lose

5

its entity in the soil and therefore remains as a sterile seed.

If you take the word *love* in the broad sense meaning everything we want and everything we try to achieve, then love stands for all our conscious activities, for everything we plan and everything we do. Christ proposes that we give rational direction to all our conscious activity. Rational is further described as that which is conforming to the Golden Rule and proportionate to the urgency of the human need at hand. By this simple suggestion Christ explained all there is to be said concerning morality and the rational way of living.

Love is the most important thing in the life of every human being. The fact that we love a certain person, thing or goal either in this life or in the next, is the reason why we want to stay alive, work hard and face the obstacles of jealous competition. Love is ever so much more suitable than force to make a person perform better and be able to take punishment. The reason for the superior power of love above external push is that, although unreasonable persons must be compelled to do things right, still mature persons should not have to be driven. Unless their education has been a failure, grown-ups work better when they are animated with love rather than with fear. This is why love is the greatest power in the world. It is behind the makings of a hero, a martyr, and a missionary as it is behind the makings of a gangster. The only difference is not the quantity but the quality of their love.

The kind of love we practice determines our usefulness or harmfulness in life. It is the reason why our life may have been a blessing or why it might have been better if we had never been born. We can stop giving our love to people but we cannot stop having the natural tendency to love. If we stop loving people we automatically become weird, because human love was meant for people. Through intelligent communication of our thoughts and rational direction of our sentiments we stimulate in ourselves the relaxed normal sentiments which are known as good feelings. In the measure that we let our love deviate from its objective of rationality, we naturally generate the opposite feelings of abnormality. A complete escape from love is an absolute impossibility. As the saying goes, "if we can't lick a thing, join it." Nevertheless the choice is ours to join love in such a way that love does not lick us. We may be poor in money but rich in love. Not too many people are rich in both. Maybe the quality of real love depends upon detachment.

In any case this all-important subject of love deserves to be examined from every basic angle. Is it surprising that the philosophy of Jesus should hinge upon the direction of love? Over the centuries the different groups of Christianity have misrepresented Christ's common sense teachings. In its place they have twisted his views to suit their national politics or further their personal aims. The many forms of Christianity which exist are the clear proof of the truth of this statement. Some of these groups have laid the emphasis of religion on whole new elements of dogmas and mysteries which Christ did not even mention. Is not the object of religion the teaching of good morals? Others soft-pedalled Christ's rigid code of morality to make it easy on themselves or held on to literal interpretations of certain passages of the Scriptures, even though their suggestions were contrary to common sense. The same feud which repeatedly flared up amongst the disciples of Jesus about who was first in command, kept on recurring not only amongst individuals but amongst the different groups of Christianity. So strong did the fanatical elements of ambition grow, that Christians lost sight of Christ's philosophy and even dropped their very name.

In the midst of this disastrous confusion and age-long digression, there is only one way of getting out of this vicious circle: *BACK TO THE ORIGINAL FORM OF CHRISTIANITY, BACK TO THE PHILOSOPHY OF JESUS.* The reason why people drifted from Christ's way of thinking was not because his philosophy was hard to understand but hard to follow. This simple philosophy is mainly recorded in the stories of the gospel, which are not biographies of Christ's life but contain the logic of his teachings. Had Christ's discourses been tape-recorded, we still would not have had the background or circumstances by which he made his points. For example, the Old Testament's (O.T.) forceful approach, symbolized by its most vehement prophet John the Baptist, is opposed to the New Testament's (N.T.) passive resistance symbolized by Christ's coming as a lamb. Mary Magdalene's humble admission of her weakness is contrasted with the Pharisees' proud refusal to admit mistakes. In this way pride is portrayed as being more abominable than the weakness of the flesh. Ambitious leadership with power and title had to be placed in opposition to leadership which takes no advantage of its position but sticks to its role of helping. Had it not been for Peter, the sons of Zebedee and Christ's examples of washing the disciples' feet, we would never have had a clear picture of Christ's philosophy on leadership. Jesus' principles of good behavior are therefore explained by leading personalities and by detailed descriptions of events as much as by the recording of Christ's words.

Our study of the philosophy of Jesus will therefore deal with the direction of love as follows:

1. The nature of love, which is divided into both egocentric and altruistic.
2. The power of unselfish love transcending the power of force and of fear.
3. The only possible way of preaching unselfish love to free and intelligent agents.
4. The logical manner of undoing the evil effects of selfish love in ourselves, in others and in the Christian community of which we are a member.
5. An example of someone who fell deeper than others in selfish love and nevertheless rose to a maximum of altruistic dedication.
6. How to lead other people interested in dedicating their lives to altruistic love.
7. How to sustain this spirit of unselfish love in the regular meetings of members and leaders.

Such is the outline of our study.

Chapter I

REAL LOVE

The Composition of Love

The philosophy of Jesus is a set of principles whose object is to bring our lives under the spell of love and our love under the direction of reason. (Mt. 22, 39.) From human nature's double aspect of rationality and animalism, Christ concludes: Life without love is not worth living and love without reason is not worth giving.

The caution that love should be directed by reason was also the meaning of St. Paul's admonition: We should let ourselves be led by the spirit. We should not be misled by the flesh. (Gal. 5, 16s.) The same thought is brought out in a number of sayings such as the power of mind over matter, the superiority of the soul over the body (Mt. 16, 26), and the importance of keeping our emotions under control.

The fact that we are able to make these distinctions proves that we are gifted with intelligence and the ability of deciding for ourselves. These are the very things that make a person. By them we have something in common with the attributes of our Maker. The fact that we are able to reason imposes on us a rational line of conduct. Intelligent conduct in turn requires that we are ever ready to lend a helping hand, although a healthy person should be able to take care of himself. There is no limit to the amount of decisions we are able to make, be they for right or for wrong, for good or for evil. Our good results will depend on how well we are able to distinguish primary from secondary needs in people and how interested we are in rendering help.

Rational direction would only be a mumbo jumbo, a phrase devoid of meaning, unless there were principles which hold in every case. We know from experience that what one man believes to be rational (for example, the Eskimo custom of letting the older people

9

freeze to death) another discards as a thing which is absurd. If opposing views could possibly be considered as rational, rationality would only be a name for everybody's personal point of view. There would be no such thing as objective moral values. On the other hand, the blind observance of the law is no proof that we have done the right thing. No legislation, however perfect, has ever been able to provide for the essential needs of humanity in an adequate manner.

If blind obedience to the law does not make our conduct rational because the law itself is blind, then we must use our own eyes and brains to discover the greater needs of people. "Let your conscience be your guide." Christ could therefore only build a sound philosophy on the principles of common sense. Some of his principles are general and must be kept in mind at all times. Others are particular and apply only in a given case.

General is the principle of equality expressed in the Golden Rule and in the first point of our Constitution. Equally important and general are the principles of priority. The health of the mind is obviously more important than the health of the body. As a result Christ urges us to be more solicitous about our food for thought (about the search for the truth and about the right decisions to make) than about the needs of the body. "Therefore I tell you, do not be anxious about your life, what you shall eat or what you shall drink, nor about your body, what you shall put on." (Mt. 6, 25.) Moreover everyone is responsible for maintaining his own sanity, because everyone has a mind and a will of his own. Our own sanity has priority over anything whatsoever. Not even the closest member of our family should be able to stand between us and truth, of which Christ is the symbol. "He who loves his father or mother more than me is not worthy of me. . . ." (Mt. 10, 37.)

Some of Christ's principles are guidelines for a particular situation. The principle of turning the cheek, for example, cannot be applied by people in authority with regard to their subjects. Restricting the body by fasting to intensify the operation of the mind is an excellent suggestion for adults in good health. Religious leaders are given the advice of remaining single so as not to be torn between the love for their family and the love for their flock. By applying, in this way, Christ's general advice at all times and his particular guidelines wherever they are useful, we let our reason be our guide. What we are saying is that we are allowing the spirit to lead us; we are not being led by the flesh.

 * Free love is enjoying one's self without personal commitment. Christian love is giving one's self without personal return. The first tries to get something while the second tries to give something. The first has no concern for others but the second does. The first is selfish and unreal while the other is altruistic and real. At this point it would be well to dig further into the power and nature of real love.

The Power and Nature of Love

Instinctively we all like to pass our thoughts and feelings onto others. Such a desire could well be called our social nature or the human need for communication. We wish to test our plans and ideals with people, extend reassurance to those who are in doubt or encourage those who seek approval. The object of communication could also be a desire to have others help us towards power, fame or fortune. Whatever our motivation may be, selfish or unselfish, the fact remains that man bases his success on the amount of support which he has from his fellowmen. The conquest of others is the natural and ultimate goal of human ambition. We all want to conquer others in order to obtain recognition.

According to Jesus there are two ways of conquering others or influencing their conduct. One is by physical force or moral compulsion, called the Gentile Rule. The other is by rendering services of love, called the Christian Leadership. Of the two, love alone respects the individual's right to self-determination. Without the right of free choice we lose our individuality. Pressure from the outside freezes our thoughts and feelings. Love is therefore the greatest power in the universe. It opens the gates to personal dynamism, namely the individual's thoughts and feelings. Love cannot successfully be repressed by force. At most, love can only be guided by reason. As Christ put it, "Do not fear those who kill the body but cannot kill the soul" (Mt. 10, 28.) Because love cannot be repressed, every country has its list of martyrs and Christianity has

11

the longest. No sooner had the earthquakes in San Francisco, the floods of the Mississippi, the hurricanes of Florida or the eruptions of the Vesuvius subsided, when the survivors returned to the place of their predilection. Even the elements could not keep them away.

Love is stronger than fear. Fear is the product of force. Force can be physical violence or moral pressure. Pressure is usually brought about by means of laws, threats and punishments. Both force and fear are contrary to one's inalienable right of self-direction. Children and irresponsible adults are, to a degree, incapable of ruling themselves. As long as this condition remains, they have to be led by others. Governments may impose reasonable restrictions on their subjects for the good of the community. Mature citizens, however, should be left free to live a life of their own. Constant interference, not to speak of the method of brainwashing, is a miserable manner of governing. Corrupt governments have more laws and less spirit, as Tacitus so accurately observes in his Annales (3, 27), while sound governments have few laws and great spirit. Christ did not want his followers to make their conquests with political manipulation and moral pressure but with the power that emanates from gratuitous service. "You are the salt of the earth . . . you are the light of the world." (Mt. 5, 13-14.)

The man who puts pressure on another without good reason has no love for the man he pressures. On the contrary, he has love only for himself. Selfish love can become a mighty weapon of destruction. Few wars have not been caused by a selfish ambition. If selfish love has been the main cause of human destruction, unselfish love can be the main cause of human understanding. Though the survival of the fittest preserves the kingdom of wild animals, the practice of unselfish love preserves the human race. Such are the principles of the philosophy of Jesus.

When we analyze love, we find it to be a deep psychological impulse, the dynamic power of all human activity. It makes us reach for people, animals, things or ideals to satisfy our physical and psychological needs. In these we look for something which gives us or which we imagine will give us fulfillment, and importance. Love is the most important factor in the makeup of everyone's personality.

12

It is a stepping stone towards our goals and aspirations. It is the inspiration to success, whether it is achieved or not. In one word, love makes us what we are, individuals with a distinct personality.

Countless people have written about love. Everybody talks about it because love is behind everything we do. We must look further into the object and ingredients of love to find out which love is harmful and which is reasonable, which leads to guilt feelings and which leads to good feelings, which love is real for animals only and which love is real for us.

The Object of Love

The first requisite of human love is to reach for *real objects*, for people and things which actually exist. When we withdraw from people and responsibility because of some disappointment in life, we lose contact with reality and become mental. The natural tendency to reach for real objects is therefore an absolute necessity to love as a sane person would.

But contact with real objects is not enough for love to be real. Love is a *blind drive* whether it be for sex, for power, for glory or for money. Even idealistic love must be guided by *reason*, or it becomes a fanatical drive. Rationally directed love must be *sincere* in *contents* and *proportionate to its object*. Love is sincere when we have a genuine interest in the other person's real needs, which means that we have no intention of taking unfair advantage of him. Pretending that we love someone can only cause resentment. How else can a duped person react to someone who is insincere? Sex without self-commitment, sex in exchange for money, sex to obtain self-advancement or procure a personal favor are not the best examples of a love which is genuinely interested in another. In all these cases the motivation is wrong. We are not doing the thing for itself or for the primary purpose for which it is intended. Secondary interests have become our main concern. If, in such cases, we are not using others for our personal advantage, than we are still guilty of a sort of bribery. We are doing a thing contrary to its original purpose. Money or social advancement are an unfair exchange for keeping others in conflict with their peace of mind. They are incommensurate values. Money cannot buy happiness.

Sincerity is not the sole quality of real love. Love is still off-course when it is out of proportion to the type of objects to which it is addressed. Animals and things are subservient to people. Loving them on the same level as people is a distorted form of love. A job is a means of family support. Having more love for one's work than for one's family is, in general, an emotional unbalance. Love can also be disproportionate with regard to the individuals of the same group. Showing preference to certain persons under us, outside of a deserving case such as a handicapped child, a sick or a crippled person, is unfair and unrealistic love. It does not preserve the proper balance between the needs of our subjects and our personal responsibility.

Speaking of the order of precedence, odd as it may seem, the first object of love is the health of our minds. The French saying, "la charité bien ordonné commence avec soi," or as we put it," charity begins at home," if well understood, makes a good deal of sense. A sick person is someone who is incapacitated in one field or other. Sickness can be in the mind, in the body, or even in both. Ordinarily but not necessarily, a sound mind is found in a healthy body, and the health of the one contributes to the health of the other. Though physical health may often be necessary for us to be of any use to others, mental health is always indispensable. Without lucidity of mind we are not only useless to others but we are also useless to ourselves. Our mental health therefore, takes priority in everything we do. When we let our minds become sick, we have lost it all, our sense of direction and of responsibility, the happy feeling of being in control and our right to freedom, the possibility of living a life of our own and of being a person. That is why we can give up everything else for a good and necessary cause, including the health and life of our bodies. However, under no circumstances are we justified in giving up our contact with reality.

Charity truly begins at home. Jesus reminded the religious physicians of his time to have a healthy outlook on life, before trying to remedy the outlook of others. "Physician cure thyself." (Lk. 4, 23.) Our first responsibility consists in setting ourselves straight. The health of our mind should be our biggest worry. The health of our

14

bodies, though often useful, is not always indispensable. Sometimes physical distress has even brought certain individuals back to their senses.

The proposed order of first taking care of our mental health applies to the members of a family as it does to strangers. It even applies to the relationship of mother and child. If everyone tries to improve his own mental health by the search for truth which is the correct picture of reality, then the difficulty for mutual understanding will soon be dissolved. Love for the truth is what prepares the way.

The Commandment of loving our neighbor as ourselves supposes that we have already taken care of the needs of our own mind and body. Generally people do not need encouragement to take care of themselves. They naturally think of themselves more than they think of others. They may feed their minds and bodies the wrong food, without any sense of proportion, but they are forever thinking of themselves. Our ego is our center of gravity. There lies our weakest point. We all think more of our own needs than we think of the needs of others. Exaggerated worry for the needs of the body is the voice of the flesh, our natural weakness and our original sin. We all need a reminder to get us out of this vicious circle. Hence the commandment of loving our neighbor.

From what has been said we arrive at the following conclusions. If the sacrifice of our lives and physical health is necessary to save the life of others, then we are not endangering our mental health by an act of self-immolation. Excellent examples would be where a mother gives her life to save an unborn baby or where volunteers lose their lives trying to save others from fire, drowning and other accidents. Love in these cases, is not only rational but even heroic, provided the individuals involved made their sacrifice freely and with complete mental awareness. "Greater love no man has than this, that a man lay down his life for his friend." (Jo. 15, 13.) Individuals, however, who set themselves ablaze even for a just cause are taking their own lives without absolute necessity. Actually they are not rescuing others from immediate danger, and consequently their judgment is not sound.

While on the formal object of love, we could ask ourselves whether

15

it is possible to love God with the same feeling which we have for people. Such love is obviously impossible. Human love is composed of a physical element called feeling as well as of immaterial elements called the acts of the will and of the mind. Having feelings for a spirit such as God is only an illusion. Loving God is strictly an act of our intellect. We unite ourselves to Him in thought as to the one whose love is free from the selfish elements of the flesh. The purpose of such a meditation is to set our own thoughts straight in directing our feelings towards people. After our directional faculties have been set straight, we go to the *testing grounds* of real love, which are people. We then try to give to individuals the amount of compassion which their real needs deserve.

The fact that we love people unselfishly is the proof that we really love God. God gave us reason for the express purpose that we use it correctly in directing our feelings towards people. By loving people correctly, we are doing what God expects of us and in this way we become his friends. The fact that we love God sincerely presupposes that we want to do His will, by directing our feelings unselfishly towards people. Though the objects are different, the love is inseparable. Loving people correctly is therefore loving God correctly. It is also right to say that the more we love people as it behooves, the greater love we have for God. Still our love of people will not remain unselfish, unless we go to the divine source of love's purification. Even the pagans, such as the Greek philosophers professing dualism, felt that man had to make the choice between the good spirit and the bad. Christ said that the fact of remaining united with Him and His Father was a necessary condition for succeeding in the practice of unselfish love.

Selfish Love

We have said that love must be guided by reason, that is, we must bear in mind the needs and rights of others, if we do not want our love to change into ruse and violence. The man who does not want his love to get out of control must keep a steady hand over the demands of the flesh. Henry VIII did not. Instead he pursued his love for Anne Boleyn with such tenacity that he identified his own

16

imaginary needs with the needs of his country. He involved all of England in his personal problem. When he obtained the object of his love, he destroyed it. Those who get carried away with selfish projects lose sight of reality. They forget that others have rights and needs as well as they. Being out of contact with the real, they have made themselves delirious. The battle between love and reason is the same as the battle between our senses and common sense or the battle between the flesh and the spirit. It is a race in the stadium of life where only one of the two will come out as the winner. (1 Cor. 9, 24.)

A child starts off in life by wanting everything for itself. It must be taught by word and example to share its toys and candy with the rest of its playmates. Otherwise it will grow up indifferent to the real needs of others. A spoiled child and a selfish person have no understanding of the value of real love. LOVE IS NATURE'S WAY OF HELPING US DISCOVER OUR MISSION IN LIFE AND OF SATISFYING OUR PERSONAL NEEDS BY TENDING TO THE NEEDS OF OTHERS. When our attention is focused on others we escape from the vicious circle of self-concern. Continuous concentration on our own person makes our mind go berserk. Altruistic love gives us a purpose for living. Rational love is giving, not taking. By giving we receive. The more selflessly we give the more abundantly we receive, not only inner consolation but material things as well. Everyone who has left his possessions . . . will receive a hundred fold in this life. (Mk. 10, 30.) Our own needs will be fulfilled by those who appreciate unselfish love. Somehow an unselfish giver will never be found wanting.

Selfish love looks for legal coverage and uses force and intimidation to make others comply with its nefarious goals. Unselfish love abhors the methods of power and legality, respecting the rights of the individual. If we want our love to remain unselfish, we must frequently withdraw to a quiet spot and examine the property of our emotions. As a young man or woman should have searched for unselfish love from early childhood before falling in love, so should everyone else frequently get away from his usual setting to examine the quality of his love. The pitfalls of love generally consist in loving

17

too much and in loving *too little*. They are found in persons whose emotions are unstable.

A mother tends to smother her child with so much love and protection that a child never learns to cope with the difficulties of life. Either the mother takes care of them herself or has someone else to look after them. With her negative attitude she prevents her child from solving its own problems. As a result of this over-protection, the child will expect the same treatment from everyone else. When this does not happen or when the child wants to scare its mother into carrying out its whims, a brat will have a fit. All the tricks of the trade will then be displayed, including deception and lying, pouting and malingering, hysteric crying and depressive moods. No thing or person can ever satisfy the one who always had everything that he wanted. Having no practice in rendering service to others due to his negative training, the selfish person has never the thrill of a grateful smile. The many good things he gets he takes for granted, without knowledge of its cost or appreciation of its value. He is strongly convinced that the world owes him a living. He never asks himself what he owes to others nor is he interested in their difficulties. It is hard to say which parent is more cruel, the one who spoils the child or the one who gives it no love at all. Both extremes tend to give the child an unbalanced personality.

Some religious leaders have given their subjects the impression that feelings and contacts with people of the opposite sex are generally wrong, and should be avoided. Repression of sex feelings, when imposed by anyone else than the individual himself, very often leads to abnormal practice of sex. By imposing an external vow of celibacy, repression of sex feelings becomes an external imposition and not a thing which mainly depends on the individual's free decision. You cannot take away the individual's right to decide for himself without having an unbalanced individual. Love is everyone's personal business, as long as love does not interfere with the rights of others. The French say, "L'amour ne se commande pas" which means that you cannot legislate love. If you do, then love becomes a comedy or an abnormal affection. It is unnecessary to go any deeper into the subject.

The contrary defect of loving too much is loving *too little* where genuine love could rightly be expected. Parents who have little or no time for their children because of their outside activities tend to make their children resentful of authority. Children get the idea of good leadership from the parents' dedication to them. Here again charity begins at home. The real needs of those for whom we have responsibility go before the needs of benevolent organizations and certainly before social parties. The ever-increasing number of orphans in our country is mainly due to selfish parents and to the equally-increasing number of divorces. Moreover, the foremost cause of students' rebellion today must again be traced back to poor leadership. Our social structure has collapsed because the majority of our leaders have conducted themselves as bosses and not as servants towards their subjects. Having no serious interest in the real needs of their subjects, they sought to please their own bosses and used their power to enrich themselves. The facts being as they are the future of our country is not quite as brilliant as the politicians would have us believe.

Yet, every man and woman alive is born for love. No one can live without it. Love is what gives us identity. It makes us a person, distinct and different from the rest of the human race. The kind of love we have is what makes the difference. Either it makes us a good person or one who is no good at all, a savior of others or a villain. If we love animals and things more than we love people, if our love is insincere and disproportionate, if we love too much or love too little, if our physical well-being and the opinion of others mean more to us than the truth, then our love is sick. The youth of today has replaced the former generation's "rational direction without love" with "love without rational direction." Rational direction without love is hypocritical leadership. Love without rational direction is animalistic love.

Unbalanced love is just as responsible for the disturbing conditions of society as the politics of bad taste. Not only is it responsible for the high crime rate in our country but also for the soaring suicide rates and mental conditions among students, for riots, racial problems and you name it. Selfish love is not real love; it

19

makes us psychological misfits in need of a doctor. The kind of doctor we need is a SPECIALIST IN UNSELFISH LOVE. He is the one who can teach us a love which does not lead to frustration and despair, a love which does not add to grief and grievance or leave regrets, a love which does not help one thing and hurt another, in short, a love which does not have to be undone. It almost sounds as if we are identifying rational love with a love which is unselfish. If so, where does a person satisfy his thirst for this kind of love?

Unselfish Love

At this moment our thoughts wander to the scene of Jesus at the well of Jacob. It was around the noon hour on a hot summer day. Jesus was covered with dust from the dirt roads in his travels on foot. He was tired, hungry and thirsty. He sat down next to the well. Deep down was the cool refreshing water which he could not reach. Along came an elegant Samaritan woman with a rope and a couple of empty jugs. Jesus asked her for a drink. As she was reluctant to give it to him on account of her racial difference, he offered to give her a drink of his own living water. She had not been able to quench her thirst for love with the slew of husbands which she had had in the past.

Besides calling himself the *living water* which slakes the human thirst, the Master also calls himself the *heavenly bread* which satisfies the human hunger. To those who hunger for power, glory and wealth, he proposes the UNLEAVENED BREAD, symbol of sincerity. He then tells them to take it and eat it, that is, to live by that for which it stands. Sincere interest in the needs of a love-sick world has always been the thing for which he hungers, the food he loves the best. "I have a food to eat of which you do not know." (Jo. 4, 32.) Jesus can well advise others to live by his own diet. Those who try to become more truthful and concerned every time they eat the symbolical bread are his bodyguard, his group of followers.

To all those who thirst for an unbridled love Jesus presents his special drink known as THE CUP OF THE LORD. Just before drinking his cup of sufferings down to the bitter dregs of the cross, he invites all others not to shun sacrifice and pain in the pursuit of love. A love which does not look for flattery, a love which is not afraid to suffer for a good cause, is the only drink which quenches our thirst for affection. Unselfish rational love is inseparable from self-denial and persecution. If we do not want to be disappointed in life, we must learn to love unselfishly and pay the price of pain. There is no other road that leads to an eternity of glory and reward. No other love is free of bitter taste. The love which bears up with the ingratitude of those it has helped and is ready to suffer persecution from a jealous world is the only love that does not harm the ones it helps. When our altruistic concern equals our egotistical concern, our love is rational all the way. Such love does not change with time, race or custom. Having been grounded on the immutable foundation of man's rational nature, Christ's love is there to stay.

The Gospel stories are lessons which have no equal in teaching us how to purify love from its selfish tendencies, and how to get along with people without painful clashes and lasting hurts. The personalities placed on the foreground are individuals chosen by Jesus who, under his guidance, transformed their native selfish affection into a love that is for real. We would like to examine these pillars of real love in order to see if Christ's theory holds in practice. In this way we hope to provide the reader with the key to the understanding of the Gospel and explain the logic of Christian living. If this logic is sound, it should be acceptable by every form of religious belief that lays claim to open-mindedness. To any given problem there can be only one correct answer. Science is one, because the truth is one. The truth is one, because reality is one. Even so, the correct answer to love or to human behavior in any given setting must be one and the same by all impartial religious denominations. Religion as well as science should therefore be free of any preconceived limitations.

Were you to study Shakespeare, you would have to start by studying the main personalities of his plays. How, for example, does Macbeth or Othello react under emotional stress? What we are saying is that Shakespeare's command of English alone does not make him the genius that he was. Destroy the contrasts and the psychological reactions of his personalities and there would be no Shakespearean talent to speak of. The same holds true for the stories of the Gospel. Were you to leave the main Gospel personalities unexplained it would be next to impossible to get a clear picture of the logic of Christ's reasoning. This is why the Gospel writers have given more attention to figures demonstrating a moral lesson than to the closer relatives of Jesus.

Many are the persons mentioned in the Gospel story as having had contacts with Jesus. We have restricted ourselves to the description of those personalities whom all four Gospel-writers have identified as being intimately connected with the main message of the Gospel. These are: John the Baptist, Mary Magdalene and Peter, the head of the apostolic group. Our next chapter will show how John's way of life was a direct preparation to the new religious approach in love. Although the Baptist was the greatest prophet of the Old Testament, he, too, had to learn that unselfish love is stronger than compulsive force. A closer view will help us to see how John became a link between the Old Testament and the New.

Chapter II

THE POWER OF LOVE
(AS SEEN BY THE GREATEST OLD TESTAMENT FIGURE)

While natural sciences broke the barriers of sound and space, while medicine, mechanics and engineering had made amazing progress, the sciences regulating man's behavior had little or nothing to show. Theology and psychiatry, political and social sciences all seemed to have reached a point of stagnation. With cargos of new books and ideas on the market, man's sanity and contentment, the practical results of these sciences, kept going from bad to worse.

Behavioral sciences are not easy to accept. In the supposition that they can come up with the correct answer to a given problem, they invariably impose a harder way of life rather than an easier one. The change from an inveterate bad habit to a good one, or the laying aside of a crutch upon which we have been leaning heavily, cannot be classified as trivial. When homework becomes too hard, we readily find fault with the problem or the idea of homework. It takes a big person to accept the truth and to face up to reality. "The truth never hurts" may be correct for the answer to problems in the natural sciences. Speaking of behavioral sciences, the truth can knock us out. Counterfeit religion, based on prejudice, magic or superstition, will always attract plenty of listeners, but tell the people that they are their own worst enemy and your popularity is bound to take another turn.

If history contains the answer to most of our personal and social problems, maybe the Baptist's way of living and leading was not so preposterous as at first it may appear. Many of our modern youth today, rebelling against the corruptive forms of authority, have imitated John's dress and his hair style. He too was a number one

23

nature boy. One thing is certain, namely, that John was big enough to be himself. Moreover John was helpful during his time in changing the old religious system of authoritarianism into a mature system of love. Our present religious leaders have unconsciously caused religion to go in the opposite direction of communistic rebellion. It is too bad we do not have more detail on the background and activity of John. Yet piecing together the little we have on him, we may be pleasantly surprised to have found a "man of one piece"!

Everyone has heard about "the Voice in the Desert." Dressed in a rough gown of camel's hair and with a tone that leaves no doubt about the certainty of his conviction, John drove the entire population of Palestine to the practice of penance. Preaching on both sides of the river Jordan and going from the Dead Sea northwards to the Sea of Galilee, he was bold enough to hold a public confrontation with Herod Antipas in Tiberias. Crowds from every part of Judea and especially from Jerusalem, the capital, came flocking to Bethany on the lower east side of the Jordan. This was John's favorite habitat. Among the populace were prominent religious leaders of the temple. John submerged them all with a ceremonial called the Baptism of Water. The water-baptism indicated their intention of turning from sin to the practice of denying their senses. Let us observe 1) the background, 2) the personality and 3) the mission of this great social and religious reformer, who had better results at his time with his primitive approach than the religious leaders of our day with their scientific methods.

John's Background

We read that John was the son of an elderly couple, Zacharias and Elisabeth. These two had never been blessed with children. (Lk. 1, 7.) The *time* of the Baptist's birth must be placed around 6 B.C.; John was 6 months older than Jesus. (Lk. 1, 37.) Jesus had to be born before Herod the Great died in April of 4 B.C.* Herod was the king who had ordered the massacre of Bethlehem's babies in order to do

---

* Josephus Flav.: Hist. of the Jew. Wars

24

part of classic literature. In short they are the teachers and missionaries of Western civilization.

Considering the gigantic achievements of monasticism, the reader will no doubt wonder why we called past monasticism a rudimentary form of religious perfection. We have seen that the proving grounds of love are people. No one can permanently run away from society without running away from the challenge of love and falling into the trap of associability. He then loses contact with the real. Permanent escape has never been an adequate answer to social problems, even though occasional withdrawal is highly recommended. As the reason for having soldiers is to fight war when war becomes a necessity, so also the object of love is to be proved in adversity. We will never become an ice-skater just merely by following instructions on skating. Our falls on the ice are an essential part of learning how to skate. A hermit is no different from the rest of the human race. Unless he keeps in touch with people, tries to help where needs are urgent and learns to put up with ingratitude, he is not meeting the challenges of love. Before he realizes what has happened, he will have transformed himself into a soldier who is on permanent rest and recuperation.

Hermits lack contact with people while monks lack personal freedom. Complete hermits may have had a less balanced love by lack of contact with people. They did not, however, lose contact with themselves. By this we mean that they were not tied down with the demands of a blind regulation. They were able to use their own judgment in giving help where help was needed and in letting their conscience be their guide. The cenobitic monks on the contrary often did lose the strength of personal conviction. In a supposition that they remained sufficiently in touch with the needs of the people (which many of them did in an eminent fashion), they still were led by the stereotype demands of rules and vows. Their love was not a personal decision. We do not dispute the fact that there have been monasteries where unselfish love was the guiding factor and where fear was unknown to the members of the community. All that we are saying is that a system of enforced rules and imposed vows leads to a veneration of the rule and to a disregard of the individual's need.

27

"The written code kills, but the spirit gives life." (2 Cor. 3, 16.)

If monastic life has as serious a psychological handicap as we have indicated, how can we account for the extraordinary results which it produced over the centuries? The answer is quite simple. The practice of religion did not reach adulthood merely by Christ's proclamation of individual freedom. Abraham Lincoln proclaimed the end of slavery, but slavery still exists today in several areas of our social living. Monasticism thrived well and had excellent results until recently, when the individual realized that the direction of his love is his own God-given prerogative. As the cultural level progresses, individuals want more self-direction. Grown-ups want to be treated as adults. When maturity is at a lower level, as it was in the past and still is in the case of children, correct discipline is more readily accepted. The O.T. was officially the period of disciplinary religious practice. Christ changed discipline into self-discipline. The sooner a society understands the greater advantages of adult freedom and is willing to accept the necessity of self-imposed restrictions, the quicker will society achieve its goal. The goal of social living is a greater amount of service and of material necessities. Besides society provides innumerable opportunities of self-development and of greater happiness provided good spirit and just administration are maintained.

From the description of cenobitical life and the Baptist's background, we can readily conclude that John had never belonged to an Essenic monastery. His character was far too independent to be held down by blind obedience, nor are there any historical documents to back up such an unlikely affiliation. John fits the description of a hermit, who nevertheless came out of his hiding place as often as there was need for it. His thorough knowledge of Scripture and the number of disciples he trained clearly indicate that he had frequent contacts with the people on the outside.

When John reached the age of about thirty-two he gave up his life of part-time hermit in order to commence his public ministry. (Lk. 3, 1-4.) What a ministry it was, even though it hardly lasted a year. Not even the most brilliant rabbi could come close to the impact John had upon his audience. This exceptional man was actually "for

28

real." As Abraham Lincoln said, show me the minister who believes in what he preaches, and his church will I join. John was that minister. The people and also the religious leaders knew it. In his typical O.T. style, John portrayed God as an angry king, ready to pounce on his disloyal subjects. Hearing his threats reminded the crowds of how God had punished their forefathers in the past on account of their unfaithfulness. The cruelties of Herod the Great and his sons and the oppression of the Roman army were still quite fresh in their minds. These had been part of their personal experience. The sinners trembled as slaves under John's unsparing words and asked to be baptized. The ceremonial was a spontaneous pledge to join the group of those wishing to curb their senses and eliminate the guilt feelings of selfish living.

With John and his disciples, however, the fear of God was not merely an apprehension of future possible harm, or a sentiment of distrust such as the people had towards their wordly rulers. John knew that God was not just a severe ruler, but a severe just ruler. His strong conviction that there existed a supreme boss watching over the good but unmerciful towards the evil, was his predominant point. There were no worldly attachments to weaken his conviction. John was sure that God would always protect his loyal subjects and stick to his promises, the biggest of which was to send a model Son to his people. As to his feelings towards God's Son, John felt that he himself was less than a servant whose job it was to undo the sandals of his Master. (Mk. 1, 7.) Speaking of faith, the Baptist was not a reed shaken to and fro by the wind of civil power and public opinion, as Jesus had put it. (Mt. 11, 7.) Without the least bit of fear, John stood up to the henchmen of the High Priest questioning his right to preach. Publicly he denounced Herod Antipas for his scandalous cohabitation with Herodias, wife of Philip, Herod's half-brother. (Mt. 14, 4.) Before the coming of the Holy Spirit, none of the apostles under Christ's leadership possessed the staunch faith of their former penitential leader.

John's strong faith made it easy for him to accept God's decisions and recognize his own insignificance. We could call this feeling humility but to him it was just an admission of the facts. The best proof of genuine religion lies in how well we are convinced that we are actually nobody. Such an opinion brings us closer to reality because it is the truth. John had certain privileges over previous prophets. He was born in unusual circumstances (Lk. 1, 7), enjoyed heavenly guidance (Jo. 1, 35), was the forerunner of the Messiah, the only prophet predicted by another (Mal. 3, 1; 4, 5-6), the only one who saw the Messiah and had the honor of introducing him officially to the people.

In spite of these prerogatives, John never *pointed to himself*, nor did he care for honors. (Jo. 1, 29ff.) He knew that titles would only impress the worldly minded but that God looks at one's personal merit. Titles tend to increase the distance between man and God by making us feel bigger than we are. John's aim was to shorten this distance, mostly in himself but also in others. The time was ripe for a closer union between God and man to take place. God's representative was ready to make his appearance. John was the herald and precursor of the new ambassador. The less a herald blows his own horn and brings himself to the foreground while announcing another, the better servant is he. This is John, example of all sincere clergymen. Speaking of Jesus, John said, "He must become bigger and I must become smaller." (Jo. 3, 30.) When some of his pupils tried to make him jealous, because several of his followers had left him to join the ranks of Jesus, John beamed with happiness. This was exactly what he wanted. The goal in training his disciples had finally been achieved. (Jo. 3, 25-30.)

Immovable as this "rock of Gibraltar" appears to be, yet some commentators think that John's faith broke down towards the end of his life. From his prison in Machaerus, east of the Dead Sea, John sent some of his disciples to Jesus with the ambiguous question, "Are you He who is to come," meaning the Messiah, "or shall we look for another?" (Mt. 11, 3.) This puzzling question could easily be interpreted as if the hardships of captive life were slowly undermining the precursor's strong faith in Jesus. Nothing, however, was further away from the truth. In order to dispel such unwarranted doubts from the minds of the crowds, Jesus flatly denied the assumption. "What did you go out into the wilderness to see?"

he asks the people. "A reed shaken by the wind . . . or a man clothed in soft garments?" (Mt. 11, 7-8.) The inference is self-explanatory. If John had weathered the storms of faith with the practice of severe penance throughout thirty-two years, he did not weaken with a few months of imprisonment.

John's Mission

After discussing the personality of John, we would like to consider the forerunner (as Malachias describes him) in his official role of prophet. The perfect accomplishment of John's prophetical mission was what made Jesus describe him as the greatest man of the O.T. "Yes, I tell you he is even more than a prophet . . . for of those born of women there has risen no greater (prophet) than John the Baptist." (Mt. 11, 9-11.) Not only had John prepared himself more than other prophets did, by keeping his irrational drives under control, but he got a greater number of people to do the same, thanks to his good example and convincing words. Moreover John had the honor of personally introducing the Messiah to the public. In this way he laid the foundation upon which the Messiah would later raise the construction.

Through his baptism of water, symbol of one's desire to keep blind sense indulgence down, John prepared the path for the new Christian way of living. By giving up his system of forcing religion upon others, John unknowingly linked the O.T. with the New. Dropping one's faith in a system that has always prevailed is not a mere trifle. Think of the difficulty Columbus had in convincing anyone that the earth was round. A lot of heads rolled when the Kremlin changed from its violent tactics to the tactics of cold war. John also underwent a good deal of inner conflict before he was able to understand the new and better approach to religion. Allow us to take a closer look at the bewildering thoughts which crossed his mind.

John's personal integrity could hardly have been excelled, as we have just seen. The people were well aware of it and that is why they were eager to listen to his words. Moreover John's solid preparation of himself and of the people made him the biggest prophet of the

31

O.T. In spite of all this, Jesus silently disapproved of John's violent methods by applying the opposite techniques. In John's mind God necessarily had to use violence. He thought that there was no other way of getting the recalcitrant sinner to change his manner of living. Why wasn't Jesus doing God's work by using the whip? Jesus now comes to the rescue of John's mental anguish. He reminds John's disciples of the Messianic wonders he has accomplished. He then tells them that if their master continues to represent God the O.T. way, as an angry king, then "the least in the kingdom of God would be greater than he." (Mt. 11, 11.) Anyone who announces God the N.T. way, as a merciful father, full of love and compassion towards weak sinners, makes God more acceptable to people. He consequently puts God in a better light. Jesus was officially foreclosing the era of the "prophets of doom," the disciplinary approach to religion. "For all the prophets and the Law have prophesied until John." (Mt. 11, 13.) Henceforth N.T. preachers must not preach with hell, fire and brimstone, but primarily with love.

Yet we cannot hold it against John, as Christ did not, that he missed the whole point of God's new approach towards the human race. To teach us the psychological avenue was the object of Christ's mission on earth. Having been raised and schooled in the O.T.'s negative system of force, John knew only "the fear of the Lord," while Christ emphasized the love of God. The old system of discipline, of coercion and of sacrificing animals had to become a new system of self-discipline, of responsible freedom and of self-sacrifice. Punishment in this life would be commuted into punishment in the next. Man-made religious laws had to cease and be replaced by the new commandment or guideline of loving your neighbor as yourself. The childish way of establishing authority by flashy dress, high rank and use of power would be replaced by authority which has the right answers and sets the good example. Henceforth the man whom everybody likes because he's truly an "honest Abe," would become the new religious leader. No one single individual would have the right to pull rank on another.

What a switch in the tactics of religion! John could hardly believe his eyes and ears. He was used to stamping out evil by force and wiping out injustice with violence: "An eye for an eye, and a tooth for a tooth." (Ex. 21, 24-25.) Christ, on the contrary, came to do away with violence. To be consequential with himself, he had to abstain from making new laws or using forceful methods himself. If even a mature government acknowledges moral freedom to all responsible citizens, *a fortiori* should a mature form of religion do so. Adult religion has to awaken in people a sense of responsibility and not instill in them the opposite sentiment of fear. Each man's moral decisions must be placed in his own hands. Forceful religious leadership by the one-man-power over another system would be replaced with the more perfect democratic rule. "What you will bind on earth will be bound in heaven." (Mt. 18, 18.) As individuals, religious leaders must lead exclusively with example and advice. In group, religious leaders may decide on the acceptability or external conduct of their subjects.

While on the subject of non-forceful leadership, we cannot help thinking of how admirably Pope John XXIII handled his own situation. He could have brushed aside all opposition to his wonderful plans of updating but he heroically refrained from any form of compulsion. Jesus opposed violence not with violence, but with suffering persecution for justice's sake (Mt. 5, 11), and with turning the cheek. (Mt. 5, 37.) James and John were rebuked for desiring to call fire down from heaven over a Samaritan village, which did not want to receive the Messiah. (Lk. 9, 52-55.) Love makes us endure violence while anger incites us to adopt the tactics of our enemy. Jesus now solemnly announces the beginning of the new era of passive resistance as opposed to the era of vindicating one's rights. "From the days of John the Baptist until now the kingdom of heaven must suffer violence," * which means, from the time of the N.T. on,

* The Gr. verb *Biazetai* is commonly used in the passive, and means "to endure sufferings or violence." For centuries this word has been translated as if it were in the active voice, thus giving it the opposite meaning of what the context demands in order to make sense.

violence must be suffered or endured, "and the sufferers of violence," nl., those who turn the cheek, "will obtain it." (Mt. 11, 12.)

We have seen that the O.T.'s form of religious leadership, with its external display of power, was an approach contrary to that of Jesus. This was the reason of John's disappointment. But there was more. The Old Testament's predictions of the Messiah were extremely confusing. They did not speak clearly of the Messiah's double coming, the first in a passive way, by trying to win sinners through love, forgiveness and tolerance; the second in a forceful manner at the end of the world, when Christ will assist his Father in judging all men with justice. Instead they spoke of Christ's coming in ways that seemed to be quite contradictory.

On the one hand, the prophets gave the impression that the establishment of God's kingdom on earth would require force. "The God of heaven will set up a kingdom, which shall never be destroyed, nor shall its sovereignty be left to another people. It shall *break in pieces* all these kingdoms and bring them to an end, and it shall stand forever." (Dan. 2, 44.) John quite naturally gathered from this and similar passages that compulsive methods were necessary to make people accept God's kingdom. On the other hand several other passages in reference to sufferings* and to "the Suffering Servant" were intermittently used to mean Christ or the Jewish nation, as in the case of Isaias 44, 1-2. Even though John himself used the Isaian (53, 7-8) expression of "the Lamb of God who takes away the sins of the world" in designating Jesus, when he did so, he must have thought of the lamb's innocence and meekness rather than of its non-aggressive character.

It should now be clear that John was in a state of confusion when he sent his disciples to Jesus. His O.T.'s upbringing and his scriptural readings had given him the impression that Jesus would introduce God's kingdom with force. So he goads Christ on by saying, "If you are 'the one who is to come' why don't you prove it by

---

* Ps. 22, 2-7-16-18; 2, 2; 35, 11; Zech. 11, 12-13; 12, 10; 13, 7.

punishing the wicked?" John was no doubt thinking of Herod Antipas, among others, who was detaining him in prison.

There are many cases where Jesus was coaxed into doing things he did not want to do. We have already seen how James and John had urged Jesus into calling fire down from heaven. Likewise the temple leaders tried to get Jesus to come down from the cross. Similarly the devil tempted Jesus into making a prodigious jump from the pinnacle of the temple. Such a spectacle would indeed attract the praise of the worldly minded who have no intention of changing their morals. Christ said, "I do not seek my own glory" (Jo. 8, 50) "but I always do the will of my Father." (Jo. 8, 29.) God's glory is obtained when a prodigy leads to make men amend their ways. Man's glory is obtained when a prodigy does not lead men to mend their ways. Some of Christ's many temptations came from evil-minded individuals; others came from well-intentioned men.

John apparently had good intentions when he nudged Christ on to the use of violence. That he had not lost his faith in Jesus is shown by his willingness to change his own approach. Besides Jesus vigorously denied the fact of John losing faith, by reminding the crowd that John was not a reed shaken by the wind. Having been trained the O.T way, the Baptist ignored completely the new and more perfect way of God's coming with love and forgiveness.

In answer to the question of John's disciples concerning the Messiah, Jesus remarked that he had fulfilled the Messianic predictions. (Is. 35, 5-6.) "Go and tell John what you hear and see: the blind receive their sight, and the lame walk, lepers are cleansed and the deaf hear, and the dead are raised up, and the poor have the good news preached to them." (Mt. 11, 4-5.) Then adding a gentle reproach for John, he says, "And blessed is he who takes no offense at me" (Mt. 11, 6), or at the new system of "turning the cheek." It was the same reproach of love which Christ would later address to his own disciples at the last supper, when he said, "All of you will be offended in me tonight." (Mt. 26, 31.)

When John's disciples returned to Machaerus with the reassuring news that Christ had the highest esteem for him in spite of his divergent opinion, the prisoner must have wept for joy. The power of love hidden in forgiveness and in sufferings now became clear to him. Gladly he bent his head to the sword of his executioners, whereby he became the first martyr of the new system of love. From now on the severed head of John the Baptist presented to the cruel king on a platter (Mt. 14, 11) will forever be the exclusive answer to violence.

John may have had a hard time in grasping the new Messianic approach and the superior power of love. When he finally did understand it, he gave his life for its principle. What is more, he had always kept his bodily needs to a minimum. Upon such selfless love Christian leadership is founded. Had the majority of the N.T. religious leaders done the same, instead of returning to the O.T. trinkets of laws and ceremonials, religion would not be in the straightjacket in which it is today. Lording it over another is so much easier than lording it over one's self. That is why the externalism and legalism of the O.T. has been reinstated and the practice of Christian virtues has been lost. In the process of all these political maneuvers, Christianity has lost its very name. "For the gate is narrow and the way is hard that leads to life and those who find it are few." (Mt. 7, 14.) Changing a system of force and of legal righteousness into a system of responsible love is not something that is done overnight. Look how many centuries went by before society was ready to give up slavery, and slavery can still return, if people are unwilling to pay the price of freedom. As long as the human race exists, the tendency will be to exercise control over another rather than to exercise control over one's self.

As John's way of living led to unselfish love and freedom in the practice of religion, so also his way of preaching may have had something to do with the eagerness with which people listened to his sermons. As a teacher's attitude often determines the student's willingness to learn, even so the preacher's attitude may be the cause why people turn him "on" or "off." When religious leaders think more about pleasing their superiors, accumulating property and glorifying their institution than about serving the religious needs of the people, then they have become self-interested hirelings. Ezekiel

(34, 8) describes them as shepherds who fatten themselves but let their sheep go hungry.

Religious leaders are primarily preachers. Preachers can be exposers of the truth or they can be distorters of reality. When preachers teach prejudice and superstition they cultivate fanaticism. Bigots are often more dangerous than people who were never exposed to religion at all. Whether superstition is of the primitive type such as the witchcraft or the voodooism of uncivilized nations or it consists of belief in magic and divinization as in Western civilization, it still is belief in something unreal. You will find that in general, hypocrites go for counterfeit religion, unbalanced people love fanaticism, but intelligent listeners take the high road where the unreal is concerned.

Many people imagine that preaching is merely telling others what to do. If that were so everyone would qualify as a preacher. Even the most competent preacher has no right to preach unless his example is stronger than his word. "I have given you an example that you also should do as I have done to you." (Jo. 13, 15.) Until a preacher has learned to be genuinely sincere, thoroughly trustworthy, patient and forgiving, humble and compassionate, he has no right to remove the straw from the eye of another. A well-known dentist once said, "A doctor is the man who tries to cure others but he cannot cure himself, and a priest is the one who tells others how to get to heaven, but he cannot find the road himself."

In our present world of hatred and of violence, where things count more than people, where the rich are getting richer and the poor are getting children, it is vitally important not to set ourselves up as preachers, unless we can say with St. Paul, "Brethren, be imitators of me." (Phil. 3, 17.) If there is so much evil in this world and preaching is not doing much good, we might do well to ask ourselves a few questions. Why is everybody preaching and nobody listening? Why are there so many groups of preachers? What was the reason for John's success in preaching? How does John's way of preaching compare with Christ's way? How do you preach real love without being a phony?

Chapter III

THE PREACHING OF LOVE

Prophets and Preachers

Wherever you find people, you find preachers. Persons who claimed to have received a direct mission from God to announce God's will and plans to the people have been given the name of prophets. All prophets are necessarily preachers, but not all preachers are prophets. Prophets have often appointed other persons to help in their specific mission of preaching. There is little doubt that several prophets have been imposters or suffered from hallucinations. The question therefore arises of how anyone can tell a true prophet or preacher from one who is false. Each religious denomination backs up its own prophets and preachers and not those of a different church. The declaration of one group of church officials is usually contradictory to that of another. The only way for an outsider to tell a genuine prophet or a preacher from a phony is to examine whether there are loopholes in his message, his manner of delivering it or in his way of living.

Jesus was quite explicit in stating that the Baptist was the greatest prophet of the O.T. (Mt. 11, 11.) The Jewish religious leaders and civil authorities such as Herod Antipas implicitly agreed. They dreaded John's firm grip on the mass of the people. In the Christian era, equally famous preachers have arisen and still come up as time goes on. The names of Mohammed, Brigham Young, Aimee Semple McPherson, Mahatma Gandhi, etc. are universally known. In the fifteenth century, Savonarola preached with so much fervor that he brought the whole population of Florence to the practice of penance. Some preachers took to rhetorics and preached with depth and erudition: e.g., Newman in England, Fulton Sheen and Paul Tillich in the U.S., Bossuet, Fenellon and Bourdaloue in France, Brugman in the Netherlands and Segneri in Italy. The great reformer Martin Luther preached doctrinal reform. He was against certain beliefs and practices which he thought had crept into the original form of Christianity. Catherine of Sienna, Charles Borromeus and so many others attacked the moral abuses which existed in the church. Martin Luther King stressed the social injustice of his people. Billy Graham brings the simple gospel message to millions of English listeners all over the world.

Famous as these persons have become in history, it is generally admitted that Jesus was able to give his audience a better understanding of the beauty of unselfish love and to spur his followers on to greater generosity. This is why we would like to draw a comparison between the greatest preacher of the Old and of the New Testament. Examining these two on the subject matter of their sermons, their manner of preaching and the degree of their success, we would like to discover the ideal way of preaching. Hopefully we will also be able to tell whether John and other prophets of the past were for real, and which preachers of our time are not. Finally, we hope to find out if preaching with love and example is more effective than preaching with rhetorics and modern tactics.

Qualities of a Preacher

Preaching is reminding a person of something which he already knows. It is bringing to his attention what his conscience or his better judgment has already told him. We all know how easy it is to get carried away with a job or a hobby. We then lose sight of the demands of common sense. The preacher is like a big brother who helps people to understand the errors of blind zeal. When factories were first introduced, people welcomed their arrival. They were a source of more jobs, income and necessities. No one at the time foresaw the danger of polluting nature because everyone was too busy thinking of more money. It is a role of a preacher to call to our attention our present and past mistakes and also the danger which lies in letting our emotions do our thinking.

Some people welcome constructive criticism. Most people hate it. The more people get carried away with their own needs, instead of

39

keeping an eye on the needs of others, the harder it is to warn them against the wrong kind of love. The preacher must therefore tread carefully. He certainly has no right to reproach other people of wrongs of which he is guilty himself. The first requirement in a preacher is therefore to *practice what he preaches*. Here we have to hand it to the Baptist. Faith in God, in God's messenger, in God's will, expressed by the observance of the Commandments and the practice of penance, were all so many means of keeping his love from getting out of kilter. His love was for people and not for things. Other people's needs meant as much to him as his own.

John truly believed in preaching by example. His staunch faith in God and in God's messenger, the Messiah, made him want to remove in himself anything that might prevent God from ruling his life. God rules our lives when we let reason be our guide. Reason and free will are our greatest gifts from God. John therefore proposed to keep sense delight to a minimum so as to remain repentant or be a willing instrument of God. When we let sense gratification guide us, then God, rationality, unselfishness and everything good go out the window. John wanted his reason to be free in directing his emotions. Being the symbolic Elijah (Mt. 17, 10) who, according to a misunderstood passage of Malachi (4, 5), was to return to earth and prepare the Messiah's coming, he even dressed like him. (Kings 1, 8.) He lived on what the wilderness had to offer and spent practically his whole life in preparing himself. Austerity had become such an important part of his life and his faith so irresistible, that words were almost superfluous. This man had complete control over himself and the genuineness of his feelings spoke for itself!

The second quality of a preacher is *not to preach himself*. In John's sermons we find no elaborate literary style, eloquent words, dramatic tone or affected gestures. John was not an orator trying to draw attention to his own talent nor did he stand in the limelight of the one he was trying to bring out. His style was simple and to the point. Much less was John an actor pretending to be something he was not. Pursuing no worldly ambition or social climb, he did not even know how to put on an act. When he spoke he had everybody stunned with his absolute candidness and self-confidence.

Tricky ways of preying on people's emotions were also foreign to John's straightforward approach. We see how guru and other religious leaders whip up the emotions of their congregations into a sort of mass hysteria or blind faith. While in this trance, the faithful see miracles at every turn. John's desire was to bring people back to their senses, not blur their thinking. Aroused emotions obscure good judgment. Besides, John had no intention of making a name for himself. Self-interest is the reason for exploiting people's emotions. John meant it when he said that he wanted to honor Christ and not look for personal glory. After all, Jesus was God's Representative on earth. But even where Christ was concerned John was not led by blind emotions. When doubts crossed his mind concerning the appropriateness of Christ's passive resistance, he sent his disciple asking the Messiah to account for his unusual attitude.

Could it be that John possessed a rare hypnotic power? Such a power would not have been too successful with the arrogant Sadducees and the self-righteous Pharisees. Suggestibility was not their greatest weakness. Without impressive subjects, hypnotism is only a waste of time. The ordinary people were obviously easily impressed. Still John always appealed to the people's sound judgment, even though he used stronger language in talking to their hypocritical leaders. In any case, John had no reason for resorting to abnormal tactics, by paralyzing his audience with fear.

Could it be that John was just a rabble rouser? Rabble rousers commonly inflate a social injustice, whereupon they become the leaders of the opposition. John was not seeking followers for himself. Although he did point out the hypocrisy of the religious leaders, he had no intention of getting rid of them by force. If John disdained all these off-color maneuvers in addressing the crowds, what then was the reason for his success in preaching? John preached the fear of God as opposed to the fear of man or of public opinion. The object of God's fear is to keep us from doing things contrary to our rational nature. God gave us reason. He therefore expects us to be rational in our behavior. The object of the fear of man is to keep us from doing things contrary to the desires of the one who is trying to scare us. The fear of God is always a just fear, because God's demands are always reasonable. They are identified with the essential and rational needs of people. The fear of worldly power is often an unjust fear, because the demands of people in authority are often unfair. Fear of God brings us closer to rational human behavior. It encourages us to do things for the purpose for which they were intended to be done. The knowledge that our actions are in harmony with our better judgment provides us with inner tranquility and peace of mind. Fear of man generally disturbs our peace of mind. It pushes us on to doing things against our better judgment, things which may be useful to one man but injurious to another.

John belonged to the O.T. primitive stage of religious development. He knew God only as a severe judge and a just ruler. He thought that force and fear, laws and punishments were always to be used when someone does not obey the law. Do we not normally use force in making our own children obey and is not punishment the usual way of enforcing the law? Truly, education, government and religion all must pass through the primary stage of discipline to make their subjects understand the need of order and cooperation. What John did not know was that this disciplinary stage should not go on forever. The whole object of discipline is to arrive at the mature stage of individual responsibility.

Akin to not preaching one's self is the quality of having a modest opinion of one's self. *Humility* makes us keenly aware of our personal limitations. It also goes along with the previous idea of doing a thing for itself, regardless of public opinion. We all fall into the trap of trying too hard to be socially accepted. Acceptability is frequently, but not always, the sign that we have done the right thing. It is the road which leads to worldly success but can also bring about a serious let-down. Generally speaking, it boosts our morale and increases our self-confidence which, to a degree, is a psychological need. Still, self-confidence can easily be deflated unless it rests upon good qualities which we actually possess. The value of public opinion therefore depends upon its accuracy.

The opposite tendency of trying to please people at any cost is trying to do a thing for its primary purpose. This means sticking to people's real needs and in the right proportion, regardless of what the general public may have to say. Great courage and humility are often required to stick to the truth of the matter, when people distort the correct picture for personal advantage. Complete objectivity rarely makes one popular. Most people go along blindly with the irrational opinion of the majority. They ostracize the one who comes up with ideas of reform. Think of how Galileo, Christopher Columbus and so many others fared in their attempt at combatting the falsehood of public opinion. As we can see, sincerity and popularity are often on the opposite sides of the fence. The task of the preacher is to try to get the people to go for the real and not to be running after popular success. But how can a preacher get others to be realistic if he is nothing more than a fair-weather friend himself?

Getting back to John and his preaching, we find that the Baptist never pointed to himself, not even indirectly, as to a church or an organization of which he might have been a member. Realizing the difference between himself and "the one who is to come" was far greater than the distance between a slave and his master, he expressed himself correctly when he said "that he was not worthy to loosen the latch of his Master's sandals." Removing the master's sandals after a tiresome walk was the habitual chore of a servant.

John knew that God had made the human race in the hope that it would follow the example and join the ranks of the Messiah. Paul went so far as to call Jesus the image of God, the first born of every creature (Col. 1, 15), precisely because of Christ's superior love for us all. There was no material interest in Christ's love for his fellowmen. Because of the superb quality of his love, Jesus is called God's favorite son. We too can become God's sons and adopted children, if our love is all-inclusive as that of our Master. To teach us his kind of unselfish love, God sent us a human Representative, an Ambassador or an Intermediary. In this way, Christ became our Mediator who reconciled us to the Father. On account of his important mission, Jesus existed in the mind of the Creator long before the Baptist, before King David or even before Abraham was born. (Jo. 8, 58.) Christ's job was to get us to acknowledge his Father as our Father, without the use of force or of pressure. By inviting us to imitate his example and by proclaiming his message, Jesus accomplished the difficult task of the divine reconciliation. The mediator had to build the bridge between us and God's unselfish way of loving. (1 Tim. 2, 5.) John had to clear the terrain for the bridge construction. Being only a demolition worker, his great merit lies in the fact that he never forgot his secondary role.

The supreme Sanhedrin council had sent an official delegation of priests and of Levitical temple-police to ask Jesus who he was. By what authority was he stirring up the people, not having received their permission to preach. They asked him if he pretended to be the Messiah, which he flatly denied. Then they inquired if he was the great prophet Elias, whom the people erroneously believed would come back to earth before the coming of the Messiah. John again declined the honor. Truly he was the symbolical Elias, although he was not Elias in person. Finally they declared that he must at least consider himself to be some kind of a prophet, for having done what he did. No one tours the country holding religious revivals, unless he believes himself to be a prophet. Again John declined to draw attention upon himself. Titles elevate the preacher, not the person the preacher is trying to preach.

In John's opinion, a true servant of God lays no claim to honorary titles or distinctions, just as Jesus told his own disciples not to do. (Mt. 23, 1-10.) John called himself a man without a status, "a mere voice" or an unimportant individual without rank or position. He was only preaching "in the desert." The desert is a place where there are no people and where nobody has any rights or any jurisdiction. From these answers we cannot deduct that John was being evasive because he was afraid of being arrested. Previously John had stood up to King Herod Antipas himself and given him a public reprimand. If fear existed, it was on the part of the religious leaders of Jerusalem. These were the people who hypocritically accompanied the large crowds of their faithful to the banks of the Jordan, so as not to be left out in the cold.

The last indispensable quality of a preacher is the *absence of jealousy*. Begrudging the good works of someone who does not belong to our religious affiliation is a sure sign of being a religious fanatic. A preacher who gives his congregation the impression that he and his organization have the monopoly on the truth and on everything that is good, is not preaching religion but only prejudice. You cannot force the customers to come to your store. When John was told that many of his disciples had deserted him to join the ranks of Jesus and that they were also administering his ceremonial of baptism, his face lit up with joy. The Baptist was now convinced that his objective of preparing others to become Jesus' followers had been obtained. His penitential program was endorsed by the Master.

John had never thought of himself as a prophet, least of all as the Messiah. The Messiah was the groom, by way of speaking. To the groom belongs the bride, not to the groom's valet. (Jo. 3, 26-30.) The word *bride* here symbolizes the preacher's success. Like the growth of seed, the preacher's success is the work of God. (1 Cor. 3, 5.) God converts people through His Son, which means that those who imitate Jesus' unselfish love, become God's friends and God's children.

The Contents of John's Sermons

John's way of preaching did not turn his audience off, nor did John place himself in the limelight. It remains to be seen whether his message actually made sense. John preached on two themes. He felt that it was his calling to announce the imminent coming of the Messiah and that he had to prepare the people by scaring them into the practice of penance. "Repent, for the kingdom of God is at hand." (Mt. 3, 2.) "After me comes he who is mightier than I." (Mk. 1, 7.) In fact, he is standing in your midst already, and you are not even aware of it. (Jo. 1, 26.) The imminence of Jesus' coming is brought out by the fact that the Messiah was in their very streets, but they were too busy with worldly affairs to have taken notice. Not only is Jesus around, but he is all set for a showdown. He will get rid of fruitless trees and useless wood as a farmer does when he trims his orchard. He cannot afford his farm to be turned into a wasteland.

The behavioral changes which the forerunner would try to effect were previously described by Isaias 40, 4-5. These moral irregularities are compared with the irregular layout of the earth's surface.

Too great attachment to worldly things is indicated by the deep valleys which John had to fill with higher aspirations. The pride of civil and religious leaders is referred to as the mountains and hills which must be levelled. Dishonesty and deceit are the crooked paths which must be straightened. Immorality is pointed out by the rough roads which have to be smoothed. All these far-out desires are a sure indication that blind drives are overrunning our thinking.

In the Gospel relay we see John at work carrying out his mission. Speaking to people with belief in God, he felt he had the right to be more demanding. He threatened the Jews with punishment and destruction if they did not bring fruits worthy of repentance. His warnings were particularly meant for the Pharisaic leaders and the aristocratic Sadducees. These arrogant leaders practiced penance only to appear repentant in the eyes of their congregations. Inwardly they felt that they did not need penance. As sons of Abraham, they were convinced that no one had the right to question their holiness. John attacks their pride, their conceit and their hypocrisy. He makes it clear that penance is only a means to an end. The end is to learn to become repentant. Repentance means turning one's heart away from earthly goals and from the flattery of people. John wants everyone to turn to God to help one another as God wants them to do. They must not go hog-wild over money, power and glory.

People are not to stop living nor must they live as hermits on an island. On the contrary, they must learn to live with one another and for one another. "He who has two coats, let him share with him who has none; and he who has food, let him do likewise." (Lk. 3, 11.) A tax-collector can still be a tax-collector, but he must not make himself guilty of extortion. A soldier may remain a soldier, maintaining law and order. He must not, however, use his power to get away with bribery, plundering, mutiny and rape.

When the Messiah had been sufficiently announced and the people well prepared, John will point him out to his followers in a most informal manner. The setting was as follows. Jesus had received John's baptism. This was the Master's way of expressing his desire to retain penance as the basis of religion. Having carried out his baptismal promise in the desert by practicing penance forty days,

Jesus was ready to commence his public ministry. He then walks along the bank of the Jordan River in Bethany, which was John's favorite place of resort. It was the day following the query of the Sanhedrin delegation. John noticed him. All excited, he directs the disciples' attention towards Jesus. Then summarizing Christ's mission John says, "Behold the Lamb of God who takes away the sins of the world." (Jo. 1, 30.) He goes on to describe his own first encounter with the Messiah as such. In reality, John had known Jesus ever since he was a boy and probably played with him. But the tangible proof of Christ's messianic role and his practical experience of meeting a man who was completely one with God became clear to him during Jesus' baptism. The Spirit led John to believe that the man in whom he would visibly see and feel the presence of God, that would be the man who would be God's Son and Representative. In no one else did he see this. Therefore Jesus is the one. Until this strange experience during the baptism of Jesus, the Baptist could truthfully say that he had not yet experienced the godliness in Christ. (Jo. 1, 29-34; 14, 26.)

The Lamb

The words of "the lamb of God who takes away the sins of the world" require a more detailed explanation. Even though John had difficulty in understanding Christ's approach of passive resistance, at least he did not attribute to the above words a voodoo meaning, by preaching that sins can be forgiven by the magic of faith alone. True faith in God and in Jesus, effecting the forgiveness of sins, is proven by the change in one's irrational manner of living. John was quite insistent upon the proof which lies in the pudding.

Also among the theologians, especially in the sixteenth century, these words have given rise to interpretations which contradict one another. Depending on whether they were taken in the literal or in the figurative sense, the change of attitude would have to take place either in God or merely in the sinner. Originally the expression was borrowed from the Isaian description of the mute lamb who let himself be led to the slaughter in order to blot out our sins and our iniquities. (Isa. 53.) The same thought recurs at the last supper, "this

47

(cup) is my blood of the covenant which is shed for many onto the remission of sins" (Mt. 26, 28), and in numerous other passages of the Old and of the New Testament.

The question is "In which sense does the lamb take away the sins of the world?" Is it enough for us to be saved or redeemed and to have our sins forgiven that the innocent lamb gives its life for us on the cross, while we go on enjoying the maximum of fun? If this were so, God would be punishing his innocent Son and letting the sinners go scot-free. Why should John and Jesus even bother to preach, if the change of attitudes were to take place in God rather than in the sinner? What, in such a supposition, would be the sense in practicing religion at all, if religion really did not make us any better?

Preaching is reminding the people that they are hurting themselves or are being injurious to others. The presupposition is that they are capable of controlling themselves, for what is the sense of admonishing those who are not? Preaching is primarily reminding the people of their duties and only secondarily advising them of their rights. Human nature being as it is, we are generally oblivious of our obligations and rarely forgetful of our rights. The preacher's job is to illustrate his principles by word and example. The people's job is to apply the given theory to their own particular case. It follows from these findings, that it is not the preacher's job to organize strikes and to be a leader at political demonstrations. Everyone must clean up his own house, the preacher his institution and the people their homes and their political situation. Separation of church and state rests upon the sound principle that in a mature democratic government one cannot have a conflict of interest without fouling up the one with the other. No one can butter his bread on both sides by being simultaneously a religious and a political leader. The Bishop-Prince leadership may have worked well in an age of illiteracy but that time is gone forever. If in our present period of development a preacher wants to get into politics, he should drop his religious title and not straddle both sides of the fence.

Coming back to the original point of discussion, the statements that the lamb takes away the sins of the world, that Christ died for our sins and opened the gates of heaven or reconciled us to his heavenly Father are all figures of speech and cannot be taken in the literal sense. They signify that by his exemplary life of self-denial and unjust suffering, Christ showed us how to become worthy of salvation and pleasing to the Father.

The underlying difficulty in understanding all these metaphors comes from the Scriptures' constant use of anthropomorphism. The Bible continually speaks of God as though He were a human being, subject to emotional changes and going from good humor to fits of anger. When angry He has to be cajoled and appeased again. But God is a Spirit. He is totally *Unchangeable*. Man, due to his physical condition, is whimsical and changeable. From embracing the needs of his fellowmen he drifts to irrational love of power, glory and things. Man must therefore make the comeback. He must keep his desires within the bounds of reason.

From blind sense-indulgence man must return to a reasonable enjoyment of his senses. From excessive craving for comforts he must prepare himself for the hardships of life. From imitating the animals of the jungle he must learn to guide himself by reason. Like the lamb symbol of meekness, everyone has to lean towards enduring violence rather than looking for an opportunity to use it. The way of winning God's grace or his favor is by having a rational control over our senses, and not letting our appetites control our common sense. Self-indulgence and violence must eventually be replaced by a love which is beneficial to all. What an undertaking for a scientist or a psychologist unless he too is a man who has faith. The behavioral sciences require more than excellent brains. The youth of our day has rebelled against the pretentious love of pharisaic leadership. Many of them have fallen into a love which is often more harmful. Only a great person does not become sour by falling into negative criticism and constant condemnation. Criticism is good only when we are willing to do a better job!

The Three Baptisms

If God is unchangeable and if everyone has to change himself, what must a sinner do to regain his justification? He must be baptized in three different ways. This is exactly what the Baptist tells us when he said, "I indeed baptize you with water onto repentance; but he that comes after me . . . will baptize you with the Holy Spirit and with fire." (Mt. 3, 11.)

John's baptism of water is the free-elected practice of penance in order to obtain the spirit of repentance. The water ceremonial is merely an external form. Christ kept both intention and form as basic condition of Christianity. Nevertheless, he added a second requirement called the baptism of FIRE or of BLOOD. "This is he who came by water, by blood (and by the Spirit)." (1 Jo. 5-6.) When a Christian comes out in the open with his ideals, he necessarily exposes himself to persecution. Suffering a bloody persecution for justice's sake is the second condition for anyone who wishes to become a follower of Jesus. Unjust sufferings make us pure as fire purifies the ore. It separates the dross and the pure gold. John compares Christ's actions of drawing us out into the open with the winnowing of the wheat after the threshing. With the fan which he holds in his hand, Christ, the winnower, forces the chaff to separate itself from the rest of the wheat.

When we have purified ourselves by restricting our senses and when others have purified us by making us suffer persecution, then Jesus will automatically baptize us with God's spirit which will then give us direction. (Jo. 16, 7.) Having removed the obstacles of clear thinking, God's unselfish love will strengthen us and his clear understanding will guide us. Our sins will be blotted out because we are expiating our guilt. The guarantee that our sins are forgiven lies in the fact that we have quit our selfish living and we've exchanged it for a life of mortification. Self-evidently, prayer is behind all of this. Where else would we discover our moral weakness or muster up sufficient endurance if not in a union with God? Where else would we find models to imitate if not in the meditation of Scripture and in the recollection of exemplary persons whom we have had the privilege to know? Our part of the bargain is that we remain united with Jesus and his unselfish way of living. The Spirit of God, contained in a wholesome way of thinking, will then do the rest. God's spirit will penetrate us as the sap flows from the vine into the branches and help us to come up with the unselfish fruits of love.

The whole idea of forgiving our enemies and accepting their injustice in exchange for God's friendship was foreign to the O.T.'s way of thinking. The Old Alliance was filled with the idea of strict justice, expressed in the principle of "an eye for an eye and a tooth for a tooth." John used the Isaian expression of a meek lamb but did not fully comprehend its meaning. He preached God's justice but ignored the power of God's love and forgiveness. He raised his voice and called the religious leaders a breed of vipers, running to his baptismal waters for fear of losing their people. "It is not man that they should fear," he said, "but God and his destroying fire." Only true repentance would save them and they had better make it quick. The Messiah was going to clean up the threshing floor. The useless chaff would be thrown into the furnace.

Comparing John's manner of preaching with the approach of Jesus, we find that both preachers practiced what they preached and neither was pointing to himself. They were both humble and in no way jealous of the other's success. Jesus proved his words, "I do not seek my own glory," (Jo. 8, 50), by the fact that he freely chose to accept a most ignoble death. "No one takes my life from me." (Jo. 10, 18.) As far as motivation in preaching is concerned, John used the tactic of the fear of God, as did all O.T. prophets, who were therefore called the prophets of doom. Jesus used the same approach towards hypocrites, but treated the weak sinner with great love and understanding. As to the subject of their sermons John preached on the necessity of mortifying one's senses in order to become repentant. To this subject Jesus added the need of suffering and forgiving or what is known as "the Cup of the Lord." "Forgive us our trespasses as we forgive those who trespass against us." (Mt. 6, 12. "The disciple whom Jesus loved" sums up the basic requirements of religion in three little words. "There are three witnesses (which testify to the truth of man's spiritual needs on earth), the *spirit,* the *water* and the *blood.*" (1 Jo. 5-8.)

Few prophets have withstood the tests of time and progress. That John and Jesus are still influencing the trend of civilization is the best proof of their authenticity as prophets. Preaching is giving advice on how to live. We know that advice of good habits is difficult to follow and is usually brushed aside, unless our advisor is able to convince us by knowledge and example that the hard way is the only way that works. The easy way of giving advice is to talk others into pulling our rickshaw, while we sit back for an enjoyable ride.

If few persons are qualified to remind others of their selfish ways of living, then poor leadership must be largely responsible for the universal uprise against structure and authority. More specifically, the religious leaders must carry the brunt of this responsibility as everyone generally looks up to them for models of right living and good leadership. The scarcity of responsible preachers must then be the main reason why so few leaders in the community are able to guide themselves or give guidance to others. Perhaps the evil of misguided love goes back further then the conditions of our times. Selfish love and poor leadership are no doubt the evil of every nation, the flaw of every man's character or the original sin of man. What better definition can one give of sin then to call it selfishness or an act of irrational love? Calling sin an offense against God is meaningless, unless we further explain that reason comes from God, whose will we oppose by going against our nature. We conclude therefore that only indirectly is sin an offense against our Maker. Directly sin is an offense against ourselves. Obviously no one has the right to be a leader or to tell others what to do unless he is seriously trying to do the right thing himself.

Selfish love is also the cause of our feelings of guilt. A deranged person may allege guilt for something he has not done or show signs of exaggerated guilt in order to divert the attention. Yet behind this screen of diversion lies the real cause of mental uneasiness. Guilt feelings can only arise from the knowledge (true or false) that our conduct has been contrary to reason. Should our past training have taught us to see important human needs and moral obligations where there are none or no needs where real needs exist, then we have lost ourselves in a world of fantasy and dreams. We return to reality by getting rid of our mental quirks. Such dispositions as partiality and bigotry, belief in magic and superstition are easily discernible as road-blocks of the mind. They prevent us from seeing the truth, observing the facts and sensing the conditions.

It is not a figment of one's imagination that some things contribute to the health of our mind and body while others do not—that other people's needs are as important to them as ours are to us and that all people are meant to live in society. Furthermore we've seen that charity begins with the individual, continues on to those for whom the individual has responsibility and ends by giving as much help to strangers as possible. It is also true that most people hurt themselves more, and even become neurotic, by excessive care of themselves than by exaggerated care for others. Pampering ourselves while two-thirds of the world is starving may not be contrary to the demands of commutative justice but it sure is a crime against the society in which we live. Contributing to the needs of others in the measure of one's capability is everybody's mission in life. Refusing help where help is easy to give and needs are urgent is a capital sin of social injustice. Love can therefore be selfish and irrational not only in the case of an individual who has just claims but also in the case of anyone else whose real needs we disregard without good reason.

Social justice cannot be fully established by civil legislation, unless the civil government intrudes upon the rights of its citizens. Communism has tried to establish a mathematical equality among its citizens but has failed to satisfy their actual needs. While improving the general condition of social justice, it has done away with the individual's God-given rights. Democracy has only been successful where it has backed up a healthy form of religious practice and where religious leaders were not building themselves an empire of worldly power. The job of religion is not to build faith in the structure or in its leaders but faith in the principles of a structure and faith in the examples of the leaders. The mission of religion is not to tell people that they are saved by the magic of another man's good deeds but by the magic of imitating a good man's example. Religion alone has the answer to social inequality, as long as the religious structure is not seeking its own glory but the glory of Him who sent it on its way. Christ told us the parable of

Lazarus and the rich man to make it clear that the O.T. concept of upholding commutative justice was insufficient for the salvation of man and of society. The rich capitalist was buried in hell because he did not share his abundance with the poverty-stricken of his community.

The survival of the fittest provides the wild animals with a vigorous species. Selectivity by thoroughbred breeding provides a domesticated animal with greater possibilities. A healthier mental attitude brings out the top quality in an animal with reason. Our thinking is sound when we give more importance to the health of the mind than to the health of the body and when we pay our debts to society as well as to the individual. Leaving the real needs of others unattended when in a position to help, may not get us in trouble with the law but it surely gets us in trouble with the demands of our conscience. Greed has turned people into wild animals and violence has changed cities into jungles. The comeback is when we realize that we are our brother's keeper because our brother is part of us. As a mother cannot turn her back on her child neither can we close our eyes to the needs of people or pretend ignorance and racial superiority. Much less can we cause injury to another without incurring the unpleasant feeling of culpability.

People who do not act rationally by treating others on the level poison their life with feelings of guilt. Guilt feelings have various degrees just as selfish love has various proportions. The proportions of the one depend on the amount of the other. Selfish love is the cause. Guilt feelings are the effect. The greater the selfishness of love the greater the feelings of guilt, that is, where feelings of guilt have not been distorted by irrational repression. Having guilt feelings is the right way to be, provided that these feelings stem from wrongs which we have actually done and are proportionate to the degree of personal responsibility. We can stifle justifiable feelings of guilt just as we can choke rational sentiments of compassion. When we suppress rational feelings we develop abnormal feelings such as cruelty, sadism, masochism, homosexuality and you name it. Then our feelings as well as our mind are equally sick.

The more rational feelings we suppress, the more irrational drives we engender. Of all unpleasant feelings guilt feelings are the hardest to bear and suicidal in their tendency. How else can it be, seeing that the wages of sin is death? When we have destroyed our own self-respect by acting irrationally, we logically hate ourselves for having misbehaved. With other feelings such as anger, pride, jealousy, we aim at destroying others. With guilt feelings we aim at destroying ourselves. The sad thing is that we usually succeed in one way or another when we do not remove the cause of our guilt. As an ostrich tries to conceal itself from its enemy by burying its head in the sand so the guilt-ridden person tries to drown out his unhappy memories by techniques which are totally ineffective. He seeks oblivion in heavy drinking, wild partying, and when he can't stand himself any longer he tries to do away with himself. Surely there must be a better way of shaking these horrible feelings of guilt!

If we are the cause of sin by letting our love go wild, then we should be able to undo the effects of sin without running away or resorting to the wand of a magician. Perhaps the world's greatest magician was Houdini. That man said that magic and spiritism are nothing but trickery. The world's greatest realist was Christ. He declared that those who do not deny their senses would never find the truth nor be in contact with reality. *Truth is the intellectual apprehension of reality*. Reality can be any person, thing or condition. Christ was so deeply concerned in helping us find the truth about love that he instituted a meal where unselfish love could be nurtured and fed. In this meal of love we search for the truth concerning the love which we should have for ourselves and for others. In one word, this mental food for thought enables us to distinguish real needs from imaginary ones, "For this I have come into the world to bear witness to the truth." (Jo. 18, 37.) Certainly the realist who called himself "the truth" in person would not propose a magical means of getting rid of guilt feelings. Then there is the problem of forgiving our enemies. If our selfish love of the past can only be forgiven on condition that we forgive our enemies, does this mean that we must put up with an insane person until we also go out of our mind? Must we turn the cheek to all sorts of violence and exploitation till our nerves break under an unbearable load of injustice? Quite clearly, there's more to the problem of forgiveness than first meets/the eye. The problem touches at the very root of the vast confusion which exists in the minds of the religious as well as the non-religious people. Let us hope that the following chapter may help us find a satisfying solution and realistically contribute to the peace of our mind!

Chapter IV

LOST LOVE

Is Forgiveness Obsolete?

Every time we have hurt someone in the pursuit of love or someone has hurt us in the same way, the question of forgiveness is brought to the foreground. The *primary* purpose of morality is to direct love rationally, i.e., proportionately to people's real needs and in a reasonable way. If everyone did this there would be no need for having to forgive. Due to the fact that most people do not love this way, morality is more often in the negative field of making repairs than in the positive field of building up. Everyone constantly uses love for his own advantage, without having regards to the rights and needs of the others. The need of forgiving irrational love has therefore de facto become the main moral issue. As physical illness is more often incurred than prevented, thus causing a great need for doctors, so it also is in the case of love. Loving ourselves more than others is a moral sickness of which everyone is more guilty than not. Hence the ever-recurring question: should we forgive another's selfish deeds and how do we obtain forgiveness for our own irrational love?

In this fast-moving world of ours, people's confusion in moral issues has reached an unprecedented climax. Some have asked themselves if there still is such a thing as right and wrong, as good and evil and if so, what constitutes the difference? How can a man of God first tell his congregation that a certain thing is wrong and a year later say that it is perfectly all right? Due to this double talk, many persons have dropped the rules of morality laid down to them by their church authorities and formed a moral code of their own. In order to prevent the people from dropping away, some clergymen have made the most outlandish concession, including the marriage of homosexuals. Still the results of these wild compromises have not restored the people's confidence in their leaders. Judging by the ever-increasing number of nervous breakdowns, unbridled morality has aggravated the problems of society rather than given it a healthy outlet. The leadership of a bargaining clergy is like the leadership of a child who has lost its parents. Granted that guilt feelings are often the outcome of imaginary evil or erroneous education, still the contrary can also be true that we imagine, so to speak, that there is no other car on the road and then become the cause of a head-on collision. Though guilt may originate from real or imaginary evil, the effects of guilt feelings on the nervous system can hardly be considered as being non-existent. Because of this necessary connection between the moral and the psychological order, between our conscience and the situation as it exists, a thorough study of how to get rid of guilt feelings effectively would seem to be a must. Correlated to the subject of forgiveness is the question of confessing our sins. Should we confess our irrational conduct to God alone, to an official judge in the matter of religion or to the person who has the right to our candid admission? Finally we ask ourselves if the admission of our guilt without changing our selfish ways is not a genuine form of auto-suggestion.

The present chaos which exists between man and God or between man and his conscience seems to stem from the conflict which exists between man and his fellowmen. We are living in a period of general revolution. University students all over the world are rebelling against an educational system which, in many cases, is highly unscientific. The leaders of systems and organizations are just simply not open to reason or discussion. Authority is accused of hiding behind its power and not behind the truth of the matter. Students do not relish the idea of having to go through a series of difficult studies and settling for a job in a prejudiced setting. The thought of being forever hampered later on in the exercise of one's profession is neither pleasant nor exciting. The conflict goes beyond an inflexible faculty and its outdated curriculum. It stretches out into the conflicting demands of society and of professional freedom. Professionals are entitled to the freedom which their profession demands provided that they live up to the demands of their professional ethics. Although the students are quite insistent upon their rights and upon the freedom of profession, they don't talk too much about a profound lack of professional responsibility. Although moral obligation cannot be legislated, professionals may not forget that they have to earn the confidence of their people and prove themselves worthy of their trust.

The fight for freedom amongst tribes and nations has always existed. The fight for rights among certain groups and classes within the nations became the fight of the century. The workers spearheaded the movement with their strikes for higher wages and better working conditions. University students organized similar demonstrations as did the seminarians who do not want to become an institutional piece of machinery. Also the press, radio and television are under heavy pressure to bring out all the facts and expose all sides of the question. Meanwhile the age-long revolutions against corrupt and tyrannic governments continue at an ever-increasing pace. In short, people in authority have been challenged in every part of the world for having repeatedly and seriously misled. Whether they did so intentionally or merely followed the blind training of the past does not alter the seriousness of the situation.

We know that wherever there is malaise of any kind, Communism is ready to take advantage of the situation. Far from wanting to solve the problem where unrest arises, Marxism is there to stir up more trouble. The whole idea behind this negative movement is to arouse the anger of malcontents of other countries to the point of no return. In this way the dissatisfied party will overthrow its own government and Big Brother Commie will rule in its place. After the take-over you can forget about your rights or you will find yourself transported to some unknown spot in Siberia. Like biological parasites who live on useful organisms without serving any useful purpose, even so Communism lives on the useful efforts of those who think constructively while it leaves its own followers in the gloom of their negative approach. When and if these leeches will be successful in carrying out their own projects, there will be no more healthy organisms from which to draw their blood. In the words of Jesus, "the Prince of this world" will not let up with his evil projects until he makes everyone a Satan like himself. While the people of today, backed up by Communistic movement, are clamoring everywhere for their rights and could care less for their obligations, Christ tells his followers to concentrate on their obligations and forget about their rights. He figured that if enough people were altruistically-minded, selfish love would disappear and human rights would take care of themselves.

Peace with our neighbor may also demand that we are able to defend our rights and stand our ground. The Roman writer Vegetius said "that if you want peace you must prepare for war."* Our natural selfish tendencies unconsciously make us take advantage of a person who is a "soft touch." That is why most people need a certain amount of discipline and sometime even violent repression to respect the rights and feelings of another. Violence and discipline may therefore be used by individual persons or by a nation as a whole to safeguard the natural law of human rights and of rational principles. Waging a political war, however, is not protecting but violating the rights of man. Where the case is not one of self-defense, destruction of life is just as big a crime whether it is done by an individual or carried out by the state.

As is apparent, religious leaders have no business getting involved in politics or in the practical application of the principles of justice. A certain individual came up to Jesus and said, "Teacher, bid my brother divide the inheritance with me." But Jesus answered, "Man, who made me judge or divider over you?" (Lk. 12, 13-14.) Much less should religious leaders be found doing the direct opposite thing of their calling. By upholding superstitious beliefs and prejudices, by playing up to the rich and the powerful, religion keeps ignorance and dissension alive. Far from helping sound judgment to prevail, selfish leaders are doing more harm than good. Religion must therefore help the individual rid himself of the effects of his previous selfish deeds. Before demanding our rights we must first examine our obligations. No one is entitled to stand up for his rights

* *De Re Militari*, 3 Prolog.

without first having kept his part of the bargain. After we have fully paid our debts and are in a position to demand our rights, we must ask ourselves whether it is wise to do so and whether it might not be better to again give up certain privileges by turning the cheek.

No one should have to tell anyone what is right and what is wrong. Isn't that what common sense is all about? If we are able to analyze the basic concepts of right and wrong, then we are also able to check out the need for confession and forgiveness or the effective manner of getting rid of our guilt. The only thing that can prevent us from finding the correct answer is therefore nothing more than personal bias. The present investigation will therefore revolve around the violations of the rights of others in so far as they are: I—an injustice towards God, II—an injustice towards a certain individual, III—an injustice towards the Christian community of which we are a member. Our main interest will be to find out if the Christian principles of forgiveness still hold in our day. The specific points of this intricate subject are apparently open to much further development.

I. Injustice Against God

Selfish love is indirectly an injustice against God. The Scriptures describe profusely the conflict between truth and deception, between good and evil, between the things a godly person wants and the things a worldly person desires. This conflict of interest is what leads to persecution. When a deceitful person sees that he is making no headway, because the sincere man openly professes the truth, he will resort to trickery and to violence. "But just as at that time he who was born to the flesh persecuted him who was born to the spirit, so it is still today." (Gal. 4, 29.) Persecution is a jealous attack by a deceitful person upon an innocent man, similar to the attack of Cain on Abel. The reasons for turning on a good person are jealousy and opposition of goals. The just person is an eyesore and a roadblock to the one who wishes to connive. Knowing himself to be no good in the eyes of God and also realizing his conscience is bothering him, the deceiver tries to gain popular favor. He will then elevate himself but throw mud upon his opponent just as politicians do in an election campaign. His conduct is in direct violation of the Golden Rule, which tells us to treat others as we would like to be treated by them. The Golden Rule in turn is nothing more than plain and ordinary common sense, illustrating the point that all men under similar conditions are entitled to the same treatment.

What makes us superior to the rest of the animal world is that we have the capacity to direct ourselves with intelligence. Rationality gives us the right to use irrational animals and inanimate things to sustain the health of our mind and body. Animals and things are there to help us and people are there to help one another. Only human beings are aware of their rights and of everything that is going on. We alone can plan our lives and coordinate our activity for now and for later. By nature we are made to follow our own sound judgment. Therefore whatever appears reasonable to us we call good and whatever is contrary to reason we consider to be bad. As people are made to live in society and constantly depend on each other for help, it would seem smart that they cooperate as much as possible wherever there are serious needs. Refusing to lend assistance where needs are urgent and where we can easily do so without giving up our personal rights would seem to be irrational conduct.

An unreasonable deed can be considered from an internal or external point of view. Considered from its internal concept (forum internum) the unreasonable deed is an injustice against God who gave us reason. This is what is meant by sin. Considered from its evil effects or the external harm which the unreasonable act usually inflicts upon others (forum externum), the irrational deed is a violation of the rights of others. In every civilized society the rights of others are protected by a penal code. In short, the unreasonable act is always an injustice against God and detrimental to its author. In most cases the irrational deed is also a violation of another person's rights.

The offender infringes upon the rights of an innocent person. Natural feelings of resentment, an urge for self-defense and revenge will arise within the person who has been treated unjustly (the law of self-preservation). Moreover the offender has also hurt himself by going against his better judgment. He is no longer the honest man which he was before and he knows it. Natural feelings of regret for having lost his most precious gift of self-respect will then arise. These guilt feelings can become chronic and are then known as a guilt complex. They stunt our normal feelings. Worry can lead to a nervous breakdown. A desire to forget the nasty things of the past can lead a man to drink or to make use of drugs. When the damage of the unreasonable deed has not been removed in due time, guilt feelings become the cause of despair and of suicide.

HOW CAN THE OFFENDER GET RID OF THE EXTERNAL AND INTERNAL ILL EFFECTS OF HIS IRRATIONAL DEED? Very simply. If he is genuinely sincere he will get to the core of the problem instead of justifying his scheming. The reason why guilt feelings do not leave us is that we are too proud to admit our failings and redress our mistakes. Everybody makes mistakes and the greatest mistake is to refuse to admit one's error. The offender makes good the wrong he has done to another by asking the offended person's pardon. Then, as proof of his sincerity he must restore the damage he has done as well as he can. Until the offender has admitted his error to himself and to the person who has a right to know, his conscience will never be clear. Should the offended person refuse to forgive after proper amends have been made, he too will be guilty of misconduct. It is irrational to continue to hold grudges when the offender has done everything in his power to restore bad feelings and damage.

With regards to the internal injustice towards God as the result of doing the opposite thing of what reason tells us, the Jewish saying is quite correct. "Who can forgive sin but God alone?" (Mk. 2, 7.) God's purpose in giving us reason and free will was that He wanted us to help one another of our own accord. If, by our natural tendency, we have hurt people instead of helping them, we get back in God's good graces 1) by changing our conduct, 2) by undoing the harm done to others and 3) by forgiving those who have personally offended us, to include our full-fledged enemies. It is precisely by forgiving our enemies who are not sorry for the harm they have done, that our forgiveness becomes a superior act, worthy of God's pardon. This act will undo any improper sentiments we may have had towards others, so that we now stand clean in the eyes of God. Just as we have to prove the sincerity of our apology to people by restoring the damage we have done to them, so must we also prove the sincerity of our apology to God, by doing something out of non-earthly motives, such as forgiving our enemies.

Forgiving those who are truly sorry is only a natural deed requiring no faith whatsoever. Forgiving our enemies who are not repentant is a supernatural deed. There being no earthly motive to forgive such as these, only an above-earthly or supernatural reason can motivate our forgiveness. This reason is that we truly believe in God and genuinely love Him. Jesus expressed the condition upon which God forgives sin with the words, "If you are offering your gift at the altar and there remember that your brother has something against you, leave your gift there before the altar and go first to be reconciled to your brother." (Mt. 5, 23-24.) To remind us once more of God's terms of forgiveness, Christ proposes that we pray, "Forgive us our trespasses as we forgive those who have trespassed against us." (Mt. 6, 12.)

II. Injustice Done to a Certain Individual

What can the offended person do about the unjust treatment which he has received? The offended person has the right to file a complaint and demand a restitution. His claims for indemnity will then be backed by both the civil and the natural law. Nevertheless Christ advises us to drop the charges and avoid hard feelings if we want God to do likewise with regards to us. Outside of the criminally-inclined and the mentally disturbed people, Christ's advice must be conceded to have definite merit. In a sense the offender hurts himself more with the ill effects of selfish love upon his character than by the punishment of the law. More people have gone out of their mind and ruined their life by not properly getting rid of their guilt than by any other individual cause. When a person loses his self-respect he has lost everything there is to lose. Because his pride prevents him from admitting his mistakes and his selfishness from restoring the damage, the offender has become his own worst enemy.

The main reason, however, why an offended person should lay off seeking revenge, is that he too is an offender who has hurt other people in more ways than one. "Let him who is without sin among you be the first to throw a stone." (Jo. 8, 7.) Even though the injury we have received from others is ever so much greater than the injustice we have done to anyone, still forgiving is in general the most suitable way of bringing the unreasonable man back to his senses. Christ substantiated his advice by forgiving his own executioners. Of everything he ever said, his last words were the greatest. "Father, forgive them for they know not what they do." (Lk. 23, 34.) The offended person owes it to himself not to let ill feelings ruin his happy disposition. Forgiving is decidedly the only way to obtain God's pardon for our own irrational deeds. In conclusion to the parable of the Unmerciful Servant, Jesus adds, "So also my heavenly Father will do to everyone of you, if you do not forgive your brother from your heart." (Mt. 18, 35.)

Forgiveness and Turning the Cheek

As we have observed, there are two parts to forgiveness, the dropping of the charges and the forgetfulness of hard feelings. We have to do both if we want to feel normal again. He who drops the charges but retains bad feelings is still psychologically upset. He who pursues the charges will always keep bad feelings alive. Still, forgiving is not the same thing as turning the cheek. In the first case we do not declare ourselves prepared for the acceptance of more injustice. Forgiving is compulsory and refers to injuries of the past. Turning the cheek is advice and refers to injuries of the present. Like all good advice which Christ gave, the turning of the cheek must be applied with reason and with common sense.

When is it reasonable and when is it unreasonable to turn the cheek? We must bear in mind that the advice of turning the cheek was not given to an individual with regards to his official status but to an individual with regards to his own private life. Christ used discipline while driving the money changers out of the temple. Leaders of state and church, parents and teachers, job superintendents and others may use certain punitive measures provided that these are reasonable. Nevertheless good leadership must always lead by example and leave a certain amount of latitude for personal initiative.

Besides the case of individuals in official capacity, there are persons who have lost contact with reality up to a certain degree. Alcoholics, drug addicts and sex deviates belong to this category. Such persons need the help of sound professional care to regain their lost sense of responsibility and not an attitude of silent approval. Because they have greater odds to overcome, they are obliged to have stronger faith and more determination. By going along with their irrational ways, we only confirm their sickly attitudes. Those who attempt it run the risk of having a nervous breakdown themselves. When we try to do a job for which we are unqualified we also lose control. Frustration sets in when we turn the cheek where common sense tells us that it serves no purpose.

To the above-mentioned categories of inapplicable cases can also be added those persons who are constantly trying to use others to their personal advantage and whose whole life has become a continuous system of untruth and deception. A Christian is supposed to be a pillar of faith and courage and not a reed shaken by the wind of power and corruption. He must know how, when and where the truth is best served by speaking up. The highest authorities should not daunt him, just as Jesus and later Peter stood up to Caiaphas.

Outside of the above-mentioned exceptions which stand to reason, the principle of turning the cheek will always be a good one. It does not provoke to anger but leads to peace. As the saying goes, honey catches more flies than vinegar. Turning the cheek tends to keep the settlement in the field of reason. Violence tends to keep the settlement in the field of passion. Well-balanced Christians have made ample use of turning the cheek. In so doing, they have generally gained remarkable victories over themselves and over others. Where one is firmly convinced that the cause is just and the people for whom we are suffering are worth the sacrifice, the benefits derived can actually become enormous. By weighing the cost of our sacrifice and comparing it with the possibilities of worthwhile results, we should be able to reach a decision which later we do not have to regret. Unfortunately not everyone is unpretentious enough to really know himself and form an objective opinion.

All through history there have been religious groups who claimed to have been persecuted, while in reality they were prosecuted for the falsehood of their opinions. Fanatic groups are not suffering for a truth in which they believe but for an error which they refuse to admit. Some religious leaders in the past have been guilty of fanaticism, oppression and acts of violence. There are countless sad cases, outside of the Inquisition, where the Christian churches were themselves the persecutors. Beginning already with the fourth century, Christian authorities were more bent on the persecution of heretics than on the expulsion of members who lived like pagans. What made things even worse is that the alleged heresies were often distorted views of original Christianity or added tenets which have no bearing on the conduct worthy of a Christian. Before letting anyone chop off our heads for an opinion which is not true, it would seem wise to make sure that we are not suffering for a cause which is purely delusionary.

In Christianity the most certain cause for giving up one's life is the fact that Jesus Christ is the Son or friend of God and that imitating his example we qualify for an eternal life of happiness. (1 Jo. 5, 4-12.) As the proof of their belief in the hereafter and in the power of love, Christ gives to his persecuted followers the advice of turning the cheek. This is where faith begins. Still most of us, especially when young and inexperienced in religion, need tangible proof of the results of our sufferings before being able to be baptized by fire. Each person must therefore know his limitations and keep his faith on a realistic basis.

Even an unbeliever who wants to have the right kind of feeling must try to have as much concern for the major needs of his fellowmen as he has for himself. If he has these noble sentiments of philanthropy, he will not be able to persevere in face of human ingratitude, unless he turns to God for consolation and reward. Christ expressed this indubitable psychological point by saying that without him, meaning without his way of life, no one would be able to go on in unselfish dedication and not lose heart.

The obligation of bearing up with injustice is far greater for the leader than it is for the layman. The pillars of the church are expected to be past masters in the difficult task of altruistic love. Except in dealing with abnormal individuals, the practice of turning the cheek should have become their habitual way of life. Just as children can easily be forgiven for their lack of attention to others but their parents cannot, even so there is a similar difference between the leaders and their followers.

Not only should leaders refrain from the use of violent means, but they should never be caught doing something which is wrong or saying something which is not true. An attack upon their way of life or doctrine should never be a prosecution but always a persecution. If, like Jesus, they are willing to deny their senses and to serve, if they love the truth and are willing to suffer for its defense, then it will no doubt be so. The leader who is afraid of persecution has no right to be a leader. Christ called Peter a Satan because Peter was afraid of persecution. He also warned Peter to beware of the easy way of using force. "Put your sword back into its scabbard, for all who take the sword will perish by it." (Mt. 26, 52.) Thus it is that the main nuclear power of Christianity lies in forgiving the enemy and in turning the cheek to injustice. Suffering injustice for the cause of truth and right is what is meant by the saying that the blood of martyrs had become the seed of Christianity.

Due to our emotional involvement it is not always easy to remain objective in our thinking. The correct evaluation of the cause for which we suffer is often a complicated matter. Humble prayer and the advice of several well-balanced persons will help us find the right course of action. Should lay people feel that they are losing ground by turning the cheek, then they must revert to the natural order of defending their rights. The correct use of force will then become the better of two evils. KEEPING ONE'S MIND SOUND IS ONE'S FIRST AND FOREMOST OBLIGATION. Violence should nevertheless be the last and unescapable resort.

Just as religious leaders are never justified in the use of violence, in the same way they are not justified by getting into politics unless they return to a layman's position. The reason why religious authorities would want to make a deal with civil government is because they are ready to give up certain principles in exchange for certain material advantages. Christian leaders however are supposed to have left all things so that possessions might not handicap their thinking. The love of their Master's principles should be dearer to them than the affection of their closest relatives. Jesus told Pilate that his kingdom was not of this world and rebuked Peter for being afraid. If this is so, what then is there for them to bargain about?

Returning to the layman's position of occasionally having to defend his rights, we ask ourselves what does a Christian do when in the impossible situation of being able to avoid the use of violence, such as in a strike, in a riot, a draft or a movement of revolt? Is he allowed to go along with the movement of active resistance or must he run away to join the ranks of the Dodgers? The answer lies in the correct application of the above-given rules of commutative justice which can also be applied to the conflicts of social justice. In the proposed supposition one group rises up against another, the employer and his company against his employees, the state against its citizens or vice versa, one country against another. In a misunderstanding of this sort, both sides must use fair play. Let us repeat once more that the clergymen's role is to awaken in the individual a sense of responsibility and not to take over by making the individual's practical decisions for him. A religious leader has no business to get involved in politics or to become a leader of a political party unless he gives up his profession. By profession a religious leader has to be the one who is big enough to always turn the cheek. Explaining the principles of sound thinking is the exclusive role of a leader of religion. Applying this principle to his own practical case is the layman's own private business. Neither has a right to intrude into the field of the other. In the language of the people, it is called the separation of church and state.

Lay people organizing a strike or demonstration must first examine if they have kept their own end of the bargain. If so, then a peaceful demonstration is entirely plausible. Should the tyrannic power of a particular country make life impossible for its citizens, then the people are obviously justified in overthrowing their government. Such an insurrection is not "un coup d'état" for political reasons but merely an act of self-defense. We admit that most of the historical uprisings have been political in nature, even more so during the last decades, when Communism specialized in sewing the seeds of dissension. The negative goal of this diabolic frenzy, as we all know, is to place the whole world under the crippling power of a Communistic tyranny. The important thing in getting rid of an unwanted government is not to have seven other devils to step in its place. Should this happen, then the final stage of social living could be much worse than the chaos which existed under the previous regime. The good people should therefore band together with peaceful demonstrations. If they are united as one man, then they can force their leaders to take notice of their just demands. In a democratic government such as ours, those who are conscientious objectors to violence should be given the choice to prove their point. Instead of forcing them to join a group of violence such as that of the military, they should be allowed to join a group of non-violence such as that of the Peace Corps.

THE NUCLEAR POWER OF FORGIVING. We have now seen how the offender can undo the effects of selfish love and how an offended person can react in the case of injustice. The general Christian attitude is to forgive. To Peter's question if he should forgive personal injury up to seven times, Jesus answered, "seventy times seven," meaning he should always be disposed to forgive. (Mt. 18, 21s.) Just as the proof of real religion lies in how well we imitate the virtues of Jesus, as truthfulness is demonstrated by how much constructive criticism we are willing to take, as faith is shown by how much we are willing to give up for the reward of heaven, even so charity is proven by how much injustice we are willing to forgive.

Charity or Christian love is the expression of our gratitude towards God for His unselfish love towards us, by loving our fellowmen in the same unselfish fashion. Christian love is perfect or unselfish because it does not seek a personal advantage. Our love is completely unselfish when we love others on an equal basis or when we love our neighbors as ourselves. The fact that we present someone with a gift does not necessarily mean that we believe in God or that our love is without personal interest. Although it could be, provided we take the other person's real needs to heart, still many people make gifts for personal reasons. They want to gain the esteem of their fellowmen, keep income tax low or buy up cooperation. When we give ourselves in service to those who are dear to us we are giving more. Giving one's self is harder than giving one's possession. Still being good to one's own relatives could be nothing more than a mere obligation and generosity to one's friends is usually another form of interested love. As Prince Bismarck said, most people give in order to receive. Providing service to those for whom we have no natural attraction as to lepers and other incurables is the hardest thing of all. Yet even here political or financial reasons could motivate our deeds.

Though in all other circumstances it is possible to have motives of personal interest, in the case of granting pardon to an enemy no such thing is possible. Political reasons can make us drop the charges against someone we do not like or force us to stimulate a friendship. Still all in all, we know that such friendship is not real. It is not possible to "love our enemies, do good to those who hate us, bless those who curse us, and pray for those who abuse us" (Lk. 6, 27-28), unless we seriously believe in a life to come. As it is inconceivable to have a natural attraction for evil-minded people, all we can do is to try to understand their poor training, unhappy background and unfortunate circumstances in which they live. In this way we can convert our feelings into sentiments of pity and in readiness to forgive. We can go one step further along the path of heroic love. By turning the cheek to abuse and by giving help to those who have hurt us, love reaches the summit of human feelings.

Forgiving our enemies is consequently the only sure proof that we possess faith, hope and charity and that we love God above all things and our neighbor as ourselves. No other thing in religion can be said to be more difficult. We could say that without forgiving our offenders, religion is only a make-believe. This uninterested and completely rational love blots out all previous irrational affection, which falls under the heading of sin.

71

The question arises whether it is not possible to forgive our enemies for delusionary motives, such as when we imagine ourselves to be Jesus Christ or God. Surely such a thing is possible, but when it does happen, people will be leading us away to a mental institution. The absurdity and contradiction of such a supposition goes without saying. When a Christian forgives his enemy because he wants to prove that he loves God, his belief in God's existence is not a fantasy such as the belief of the person who thinks that he is God. Although we have no physical proof of God's existence, intellectual or metaphysical evidence we have galore. Our belief is not in something which cannot possibly be true, but in something without which no thing has any reason to exist. Our faith is therefore both rational and justifiable.

Recalling the case of Mahatma Gandhi, who resisted violence with passive endurance and held numerous hunger strikes, we must admit that few leaders have had equal impact on such large numbers of followers. In the practice of penance and in suffering for his ideals, he is one of the greatest men that the world has ever known. Although penance is extremely important to gain control of our personal drives, nevertheless it defeats the purpose when it becomes a danger to our health. As a result we fail to see how a hunger strike can be considered to be a justifiable means to an end. For a Christian both the end and the means to the end must remain within the bonds of reason.

In the O.T. an animal was sacrificed to expiate the irrational deeds which man had committed. As a result, the people got the impression that God's forgiveness was automatically granted by the ritual of a sacrifice or with a service of atonement. In reality the sacrifice of an animal was only intended to remind the sacrificer that he must sacrifice his own bad habits. In the N.T. the symbol is generally omitted so that the moral lesson might better stand out. The guilty person must no longer revenge himself on an irresponsible animal nor must his feelings of guilt be directed towards taking his own life. On the contrary the destructiveness of guilt must be directed towards the cause of injustice, which lies in being over-indulgent to ourselves. The negative requirement of obtaining God's

72

forgiveness is therefore that we sacrifice our selfish pleasures. The positive requirement is that we sacrifice our right to revenge. The symbol must make room for the real. The sacrifice of things must be replaced with the sacrifice of self. By forgiving our enemies and dropping hard feelings we become the sacrificial lamb. Our completely rational love neutralizes all previous irrational affection. In the N.T. forgiving our enemy, loving God, Christian love and obtaining God's pardon all four mean the same identical thing.

Until now we have seen how an act is internally wrong because it is contrary to the common sense which God has given us. We have followed the ill effects of this act in the person guilty of selfish love (the offender) and in the person affected by selfish love (the offended). The offender can nevertheless undo the internal and external effects of his irrational deed. The offended person can also benefit from the injustice received by the bestowal of pardon. In this way he becomes a better person and deserving of God's love.

We have now covered the subject of selfish love for as far as such love is an injustice against God and an injustice against a certain individual. It remains for us to see how selfish love affects a Christian community. If Christians do not live by the standards of their founder, they are not only useless to themselves as a group but also useless to the rest of the nation. Their mission is to be "the salt of the earth" and revive the good spirit amongst the people. A free nation such as ours, which gives religion liberty and support, has the right to expect that religious leaders come up with satisfactory results.

III. Injustice to the Christian Community

Jesus gave the name of church to a group of followers who freely sought community life with a minimum of personal indulgence and a maximum of altruistic dedication. The main object of all members and especially of the leaders is complete dedication to the truth. In this way everyone would have a strong grip on reality and a healthy outlook on life. The secondary interest of providing for the indispensable needs of the body was mainly the responsibility of the mass of the lay people. Everyone should be ready to suffer for his ideals

73

and use the principle of passive resistance as much as possible. "If any man wants to become my disciple, let him deny himself, and follow me." (Mat. 16, 24.) As the majority of the people in the world can hardly be expected to have the same high degree of dedication which Jesus required of his disciples, the Master described his followers as his small flock (pusillus grex). They were the salt of the earth who must carefully preserve the salifying power of their good spirit, if they are to be useful to the rest of society. Christ also calls them the lamp of the world. Their good deeds of rational love are meant to throw light on those who live in selfish darkness. A great closeness should exist amongst the members and an extraordinary readiness to stand by each other in all their needs. Insincerity is their worst enemy because it is used to cover up the self-interest of certain individuals. Deceit brings distrust and destroys the good spirit of mutual understanding. In a Christian community the deceitful person is like a wolf who disguises himself as a lamb in order to be able to ravage the flock.

Jesus had just told his followers the parable of the hundredth sheep which left the fold and went astray. He went on to talk about the wolf that crept into the fold disguised as a lamb. "If your brother sins against you(r) community, go and tell him his fault, between you and him alone." (Mt. 18, 15a.). Paul (Gal. 6, 1) warns us that this admonition must be done in all meekness because the admonisher never knows when he too will be guilty of a similar mistake. Should a private warning given with the utmost of kindness fail to stimulate the delinquent with feelings of remorse then the admonisher should enlist the help of other exemplary persons. If a combined admonition remains unsuccessful, then the whole community should try to convince the man of his unchristian behavior. In the event that the unanimous approval of the whole congregation produces no results, then the religious leaders must separate the impenitent sinner. The man will be dealt with in the same way as the Jewish religious leaders dealt with the heathens and the tax-collectors. In the early times of Christianity, the practice was to expel or to excommunicate hardened sinners on account of bad conduct. There was no such thing at first of getting rid of someone for a political count of heresy. Ill conduct is what keeps people apart in practical living. Heresy is what keeps people apart in theoretical discussions. The first separation is real. The second is artificial.*

Then Matthew 18, 18 concludes his story on how to deal with unedifying members of the church by literally spelling out the words which give to leaders the power of excommunication. Jesus uses the introductory words, "truly I say to you," indicating that a statement of importance is to follow. Then come the words which give to leaders the right to bind all sincere followers in one united group and to throw the hypocrites out. "Whatever you bind on earth shall be bound in heaven and whatever you loose on earth will be loosed in heaven." John the Evangelist (20, 22-23) places the conferral of this power after the Resurrection. Using similar words he said, "Receive the holy Spirit. Whose (public) sins you shall forgive they are forgiven, whose sins you shall retain they are retained." Logically the bestowal of power would be expected to have taken place after the Resurrection. The reason why Matthew placed these words where he did was that he wanted to contrast the apostles' dispute for personal rank in the beginning of the chapter with the bestowal of collective power later on.

According to Matthew 16, 18-19, Jesus had previously promised Peter at Caesarea Philippi the supreme power of the keys. The occasion which elicited this promise was when Peter had made a public profession of faith in the Messianity of Jesus. When the time was there to carry out his promise, Christ did not confer the promised power on Peter alone but on the group of the disciples united in body. The inference is not hard to grasp. In order to direct the religious community of his church in such a way that the gates of hell would not prevail against it, the leaders must have the same faith in Jesus which Peter had in his Master. Unless all leaders are convinced that Christ's way of living is God's way of loving, political

* See Encyclopedia on Penance in Public, which later developed into private confessions due to relaxation of early Christian principles.

reasons will invariably influence their decisions even though they abide by the majority of the vote. The second conclusion need hardly be explained. In a society which is run by good will and by idealism, no single person can lord it over another, without destroying the goodwill spirit and replacing it with fear.

Both Jesus and the Evangelists clearly understood the great danger inherent to the exercise of power. Its recipients would readily consider their authority as something given to them on a permanent basis. They would stop considering themselves on trial or taking a distrustful attitude against their personal feelings. Prayer and watchfulness would be thought of as advice for those who did not have the title of leaders. To make it clear that no one had the monopoly on Jesus' backing or the right to the keys on a lifetime basis, both Jesus and the Evangelists will constantly stress the weakness of the apostles, and particularly that of Peter. The spiritual leader's right of office must depend on the leader's correct disposition and on the fact that his example cannot be reproached. Unlimited trust in God and distrust in one's self are the absolute requisites of a leadership which is not merely Christian by name.

Peter deserves praise for having understood that Jesus is "the" Son or friend of God. The perfect friend of God is the man who loves others without expecting an earthly bonus in return. The only reward which Jesus did have was of a psychological nature and inseparable to every one of our deeds. From the knowledge that our altruistic love has been completely unselfish we obtain a peace of mind which the world cannot give. Personal satisfaction comes to the man who knows that he has helped, where the needs of people are the greatest. It would have been arrogance on Simon's part to claim that he had discovered the epitome of human love by himself and found it to be present in Jesus. Someone has helped Peter in making his discovery. Had Peter followed the normal aspirations of all flesh and blood, he would not have known enough about love to look for perfect love in Jesus, nor would he have known how wonderful unselfish love can actually be. Pure altruistic love without some small degree of personal gain could not possibly have turned him on.

Materialistic people are bent on earthly gains and unfortunately the majority of the church-goers belong to this category. In their pursuits, they do not differ from atheists or agnostics who profess to have no faith at all. In a way, non-believers are more consequential in their claims then worldly-minded believers. What good is it to say that we believe in God, if our pursuits are mainly things of this life and not of the next? Pecuniary gain does not excite them, but they sure love the places of honor at a feast and want to be considered the number one benefactors of society. Only the man who sincerely believes in the hereafter can help others regardless of personal gain or public opinion. His motive is the reward of the life to come. Faith in the fact that there is a God makes us want to help people who do not know what gratitude is. Love of God or admiration of God's unselfish love encourages us to put pure altruistic love into practice. Understanding and courage are the result of focusing our thoughts on the One who alone can make it all worthwhile.

Taking credit for something we have done supposes that we've done this thing all by ourselves, without the help of anyone else who showed us the way. People who do not put their trust in God as Jesus did, will necessarily go the selfish way of every human being and pursue the self-interests of all flesh and blood. Taking Christ into the boat of our lives and trying to have equal feeling for the essential needs of others is the only way to avoid our natural weakness. If we want to lose our bias and get rid of our selfish traits, we necessarily have to follow the principles of Jesus, because there is no other way of doing it. A sane person cannot do a difficult thing without some sort of motivation. If he does not have an earthly motive he is bound to have an above-earthly reason. In the same way, we cannot remain faithful to the continuous practice of unselfish love unless Christ's principles become our principles. What is true of the citizens in the country is true of the Christians among themselves and is also true of everyone with regards to Jesus, "United we stand, divided we fall." When we break up the natural closeness which Christians are supposed to have, we automatically turn to where everyone is out for himself. As Jesus was the one who promised us a reward and showed us how to earn it, the credit is all his when our love has the right kind of sparkle. We have only furnished the material. He gave to the material the sublimity of its form.

In Chapter 16, Matthew places Peter's honorary confession after Christ's severe warning not to become self-inflated leaders like the Pharisees and Sadducees. Jesus compares the activity of these self-righteous ministers with the bloating effect of leaven. Then right after Christ's unique compliment for Peter follows the strongest possible rebuke. Addressing Peter as a Satan, Christ tells him "that he is more concerned about the safety of his life than about the plans of God." Peter recognized Jesus as the Messiah. However, when it became clear to him that he might have to suffer for his own messianic principles, he shied away like a coward. Denouncing the corrupt religious leaders in Jerusalem and taking the rap for such brazen denunciation were the inescapable roles of God's representatives on earth. Obviously Peter was not prepared for a showdown of his personal convictions. To his greatest regret he had to admit to himself that he was no more than a fair-weather friend.

Letting Peter sink into the water and pulling him out again was another one of Christ's wise techniques by which he made Peter aware of his weakness for boasting. Without the support of Christ's principles and the encouragement of those who loved them, no one can possibly expect to persevere in the difficult task of unselfish dedication. (Mat. 14, 29-31.) The same thought is brought out in the stilling of the storm. Were it not for Jesus' presence and his confidence in his Father's protection, the disciples would have lost their heads and drowned in their own boat, regardless of their experience at sea. (Mt. 8, 23-26.)

Jesus no doubt intended Peter to be his foremost leader but he did not want him to lead the worldly way with power and title. A Christian leader should not put pressure on another. He should reserve his pressure for himself. Instead of having too much confidence in his own wisdom, his confidence should be in what the worldly-minded consider to be folly. If he does not learn to idolize Christ, naturally he will go back to the idolization of himself. As first amongst equals, the devil was out to make Peter fall. There is no doubt that he would not have been successful to the point of sifting Peter as useless chaff from the rest of the wheat, had Jesus not prayed to save him from a certain downfall. Then, knowing that Peter still hadn't learned his lesson, Jesus foretells his friend that he would go as far as to deny publicly to have ever known him. In spite of Simon's protest that this would never happen, the apostle had to admit to his shame that his boastfulness had made the predictions turn out to be true. (Lk. 22, 31-34.)

The miraculous catch of fish in the Tiberian sea was another proof that science and human wisdom are not quite enough to convince the people to live a good life. If the disciples followed their own wisdom in preaching, they would soon find out that they are wasting their time by working in the dark. On the other hand, should they adorn their nets with faith in God and with unselfish love for their neighbor instead of trying to win people with fanatical proselytism, then their nets and boats would be too small to hold all the fish! Up to the very moment of his Ascension, Jesus reminded his over-confident leader of the fallibility of every human being. Three times he repeated the same question to Peter, as if his promise was only as good as his deeds, "Simon, son of John, do you love me?" (Jo. 21, 1-17.)

The conclusions to the foregoing lessons are unmistakably clear. Jesus did give the external power of excommunication to church leaders as a group. The ravage which the insidious wolf in sheepskin inflicts upon the community has to be removed like gangrene from the body. The leaven of selfish love will otherwise dissolve the mutual bonds of trust and dedication. These are the ties that keep a group of sincere people united as one. Power over others when in the hands of a single person disbands love and instils fear. Christ came to disband fear and to instil love. He could not therefore let one individual lord it over another. Moreover, religious leaders must be conscious of their own weakness, forgive the frailties of human nature and reserve excommunication for a case of an impenitent transgressor. Did not Jesus go after the weak sinner? Distrust in self and trust in the power of unselfish love are the only means of coming out victorious. Most People like Peter, Paul and Mary (Magdalene) learn the hard way.* Hence Christ reminds us to "watch and to pray lest we succumb by falling into temptation." (Mt. 26, 42.)

* The difficulty about the hard way is that the damage can easily become total and permanent, both for the person who commits the blunder as for those whom he has injured.

Chapter V

REDEEMED LOVE

As the preacher's personal example is more effective than his most eloquent sermon, so also the example of a spectacular conversion is more convincing than volumes of theory on the logic of forgiveness. The positive approach to morality is to direct love towards human needs in a rational way. Those who go about religion by loving their neighbor with their whole mind, with their whole soul, and with all their strength do not need to be forgiven. However, few people outside of perhaps Jesus were able to live up to the demands of religious perfection. Not only are we all selfish at times, but we are also more apt to learn the need of altruistic love from the bad effects of selfish love. The bigger our mistakes of selfish love the more we see the need of giving ourselves without personal gain. If we are sincere we will also be interested in obtaining the perfection of love. Our aim will then be to discover and admit those things which prevent us from reaching that perfection. Most people and poor leaders of religion greatly fall short of the expected measure of ordinary sincerity. They exclude themselves from ever discovering the satisfying happiness of a perfect love. When we admit our blunders we are on the road to forgiveness. The next step is to forgive in order to be forgiven. Admission of our mistakes and forgiveness are therefore de facto the main moral issue. Does it surprise us then that forgiveness is the gospel's most prominent theme?

It takes great courage to admit one's faults and blunders. The greater the blunders which we have committed the harder it is to overcome one's shame. When elements of puritanic show and Pharisaic rigorism have crept into our past religious training then the difficulties can easily become unsurmountable. Courageous admission of mistakes helps us to turn self-love into altruistic love. There are times when only a tragedy can make us sit up and think. Some people learn only from tragic experiences where the damage is irreparable and the ability to change practically impossible. Hard experiences are not experiences which are hard to find. Somehow we run into bad luck experiences without even going out of our way. Rasputin, who was known as the mad monk, believed in doing things the hard way. He thought that if one fell deep enough in immorality, disgust would then take over. The thing about Rasputin's theory is that a smart person does not have to go over the Niagara Falls to be convinced that rapids are dangerous. However should we make the mistake of letting ourselves be dragged over these falls and manage to survive, everyone would naturally be intrigued to know the secret of our courage and success.

A certain veteran of World War II claimed that he had jumped out of a plane at a height of two thousand feet with a parachute that did not open. Interesting as this story may seem to older people, the incredulous youth of our day would hardly be impressed. They have heard so many stories of what would seem to be physically impossible that they are inclined to believe the opposite of what their closed-minded elders have to say. There is an irresistible trend today of exploring the unknown and finding out things for one's self. With the use of all sorts of drugs among other things, youngsters have undergone experiences which were completely unknown to their parents. Their experiments have often caused irreparable damage to the nervous system and loss of self-control, not to speak of indescribable anguish. The funny thing about this situation is that youngsters don't believe in the seriousness of danger, even when warned by their very close friends. Just as the previous generation closed their ears to the ill effects of alcohol and venereal disease, so the present generation lends a deaf ear to a constant warning. Actually most people are much too busy trying to keep their own heads above water to listen to continual "bewares." When their attitude is constructive, people are looking for a solution to their problem and not for an example of failure. Stories of defeat are depressing and negative in approach. Stories of success are uplifting and agreeable to a person with a positive outlook. We figure that if a man with greater difficulties was able to succeed, we also stand a good chance of success.

Selfish love is everybody's weakness. Some people are more selfish than others. The circumstances of life have much to do in making us good, bad, selfish or unselfish. Besides what is morally good in one culture may be immoral in another. The habits and custom of people help to determine our concept of morality. Though the Golden Rule is an objective norm of moral conduct, its interpretation is nevertheless subject to the biased views of the interpreter. Had we been raised in an uncivilized country, our concept of morality would be quite different from what it is today. In spite of our Western civilization, the white man was less honest than the uncivilized Indians. What we call education is the development of the mind and has no direct bearing on the formation of character. Have not civilized countries, especially of Western Europe, been known for their exploitation of backward colonies? Science is more often used for power and greed than for helping people in distress. Social injustice is the result of people who are all brains and no heart.

Generalities of this sort all lead to an inevitable conclusion. It does not matter too much which is our nationality, culture, or background. As long as we help people instead of hurting them, our conduct is rational. By nature everyone is selfishly inclined, one person moreso than another. Smart people learn from previous mistakes. When mistakes have been amended, it is irrational to blame a person for his past. Condemning a person who has corrected his mistakes is the "holier than thou" attitude. An unwed mother who takes proper care of her child deserves more sympathy than the proud Pharisee who has never loved anyone but himself. Countless persons have sunk deep in immorality but subsequently became outstanding examples of unselfish love. Contrary to what Rasputin may have thought, the phenomenon of total conversion only takes place when mistakes were made without malice or premeditation.

The specific role of the Gospel is to prove that "God so loved the world that He gave His Son" to teach us the correct way of loving people. (Jo. 3, 16.) Consequently, when this model of human behavior made his appearance, he naturally went in search of the "lost sheep" or the person whose mind and heart were sick. Jesus wanted to teach the sinners how to love without harming themselves or others. In the Gospel, Mary Magdalene was the lost sheep loving all the wrong things in life. At her time she was the biggest sinner who succeeded in developing a maximum of unselfish dedication. It is not important who captivates our admiration, as long as this person is able to turn us from our selfish ways. Sometimes the one whom we have known personally as a father or mother may make a deeper impression on us than someone we read about in a book. We have chosen Mary Magdalene because the Gospel has chosen her as the best example of that time. Moreover, much like the present generation, Mary got lost with the practice of free love. Gleaning together the details of her life from implicit facts and allusions in the Gospels, we may be happily surprised to find out that human nature has not changed since that time.

In the supposition that Mary Magdalene is none other than Mary of Bethany, sister of Martha and Lazarus, a number of things will readily fall into place. Mary left her home of Bethany to live in Magdala, borough of the capital city of Tiberias. When a country girl leads a loose life in the big city and returns to her village, her townfolks are likely to give her the nickname of the place where she led a life of dissipation. Herod Antipas had built the new capital in 20 A.D. on the western shore of the Galilean Sea and named it after the presiding emperor (Tiberius, 14-37 A.D.). The city naturally became the home of the courtiers and of the well-to-do. People who are interested in fast living go where the money is plentiful.

Perfume and Charms

What else would Mary be doing as a public sinner in the outskirts of the capital if not running a business of perfume and of charms? The one goes with the other. Mary's ample supply of perfume seems to be an excellent proof of the given assumption. Aromatic products were very costly in those days. The alabaster flask, containing a pound (327 gr.) of Indian Nardus-plant extract, which Mary poured over the head and feet of Jesus in Bethany, was estimated at 300 pence. (Jo. 12, 5.) When we consider that a laborer only earned one pence a day, or about 25 cents in our money, then this perfume represented roughly the whole year's wages of an ordinary laborer. This is why perfume was often diluted with oil, especially for the anointing of the feet, just as we dilute perfume with the spirits of colognes. People in those days traveled mostly on foot and wore sandals without stockings. When a guest of honor entered a house, the host would first wash his guests' feet and then massage them with oil or with perfumed oil, if he could not afford the pure extract. Perfume was also applied to the guests' hair just as women of today rub it behind their ears. Apparently perfume was a lucrative business where bacchanalia were everyday occurrences. It was no doubt at one of these royal parties that our courtesan Mary Magdalene met Joanna, the wife of Chuza. (Lk. 8, 2-3.) Chuza was Herod's "epitropos" or the trusted administrator of his personal affairs.

In complement to her business in perfume, Mary also worked her charms in the milieus of debauchery and revelry. The long story of how Herod Antipas, tetrach of Galilea and Perea (4 B.C.-A.D. 39), while visiting Rome seduced Herodias, wife of his half-brother Herod-Philip, then married her and sent his own wife back to her father, King Aretas; of how Herodias had such intense hatred for the Baptist denouncing her second marriage that she enlisted her daughter Salome (about fifteen years old) to perform lewd dances before her inebriated husband (the whole plan was to trick Herod into making a wild promise by which she could demand the beheading of the Baptist)—this long and complicated story gives us a vague picture of the immoral environment in which Mary was wasting her time.

In order to be successful in her business, Mary must have had an attractive figure and a pleasant personality. Like all single girls of her time, and most girls of today, she wore her beautiful long hair loosely. Her irresistible charms also became her downfall. Mary fell to the lowest possible moral depths, so low that in all Christian circles, she was known as "the woman out of which Jesus had driven seven devils" (Lk. 8, 2; Mk. 16, 9.), the word *seven* being a colloquialism for "a large number" or "a great deal" of evil. Mary may have started her business with good intentions, but this type of business is so risky that those who run it trap themselves most of all.

The Conversion of a Sinner

Where did Jesus pull Mary out of the mire into which she had fallen? The exact time and place of Mary's conversion is not known. Luke 8, 2-3, gives the names of certain women who accompanied Jesus and his disciples on their missionary trips and took care of their food and clothing. He says that these women were healed from either evil spirits or sickness and perhaps from both. According to the wording, it would seem that Joanna was healed from a physical illness and that her friend Mary was cured from a life of prostitution. Whatever it was that caused Mary and Joanna to abandon their mundane life, it certainly must have been a very extraordinary happening.

Not knowing the exact occasion which led to the conversion of this conspicuous sinner, it would seem that the evangelists, who made so much of Mary Magdalene, would at least have to tell us where this singular conversion had taken place. Of the four Gospel writers, Luke lays particular stress on the saving qualities of Jesus. He alone has the parable of the Prodigal Son, (15, 11-32), and with Matthew, the story of the Lost Sheep (15, 1-7). Only Luke has the historical conversions of "the public woman" (7, 36-50), and of "Zachaeus, the Tax-Collector" (19, 1-10). Luke gives ample detail of how the Scribes and Pharisees publicly criticize Jesus for being friendly with sinners and tax-collectors with whom he ate and drank.

In answer to these accusations, only Luke records the rebuttals of Jesus. "Those who are well, have no need of a physician. Contrarily, those who are sick, do. I have not come to call the righteous, but sinners to repentance." (Lk. 5, 3-32.) "For the Son of man came to seek and to save what is lost." (Lk. 19, 10.) Luke's favorite theme, that the main goal of the Gospel and the principal aim of Jesus was the conversion of sincere sinners, is confirmed by the drawings and the paintings on the walls of the catacombs. These frescos invariably represent Jesus not in his physical traits (which the painter could not possibly have known,) but as a symbol of the main theme of the Gospel's story. Jesus is constantly represented as the Good Shepherd with the lost sheep on his shoulder.

Could it be, that in the description of "the Public Woman" Luke is giving us the actual conversion of Mary Magdalene? Somewhere in Galilee a party was given in honor of Jesus during the early part of his public ministry. Simon the Pharisee, a notable citizen, had invited the Master and other personalities to his house for supper. On an occasion such as this, the doors of the house were left open for the guests to enter. A well-known public woman appears on the scene. As she approaches Jesus from the rear, she throws herself at his feet, which she bathes with her tears, pouring the whole contents of an alabaster flask over them. Luke mentions no name because everyone knows this public woman only too well. Why press the embarrassment?

On the other hand we know that John the evangelist wrote his Gospel in the second generation after Christ, namely about 98 A.D. He added names and details to his stories, which the other evangelists had intentionally omitted. Most of the persons involved in the Gospel stories were still alive at the time that the Synoptics were written. It was therefore superfluous to add the public woman's name to the scene which took place in the house of Simon the Pharisee or to identify Mary Magdalene with Mary of Bethany. At the end of the *second generation*, however, most of the witnesses had died, and oral tradition had become quite blurred. The meaningfulness of the Gospel stories was becoming impaired by lack of names and details. This is why John added the missing links.

It may seem to the reader that proving the identity of Mary Magdalene with Mary of Bethany and the Penitent Woman is a drift from our topic on the philosophy of Jesus. Still we must bear in mind that Christ's basic principle of overcoming our inborn trend for selfish love was becoming obscure when the practical example illustrating this principle had been distorted. The correct exposition of the sinner-saint figure could therefore be of primary importance.

In the earlier centuries, the original Latin tradition had always upheld that all three women were the identical same person. Later on the Pharisaic interpretation, going back to the middle ages, was guilty of differentiating the pious Mary of Bethany from both Mary Magdalene and the converted woman in the house of Simon the Pharisee. It would be unacceptable to the Pharisaic point of view that Jesus would have befriended a big sinner, no matter how thoroughly the former sinner may have changed his ways. Association with a past sinner looks bad, especially to those who do not forgive others and who spend their lives with negative criticism. The aprioristic thinking of Pharisaism has destroyed the true image of the Gospel, which lies in forgiving others in order to obtain God's pardon. This is why we are spending all this time in retracing the correct image of the Gospel's practical example. In two simple points we would like to establish that: a) the Public Woman is Mary of Bethany, and the next that b) Mary of Bethany is Mary Magdalene.

The Public Woman Is Mary of Bethany (According to John)

Comparing the procedures used by the Public Woman in the house of Simon the Pharisee with those of Mary in the house of Simon the Leper, we note an amazing similarity. Both women make extravagant use of precious ointment in anointing, not the head, but the feet of Jesus, which they dry with their long hair. We ask ourselves, from where could this abundance of perfume have come, if not from someone who had been running such a business? However, the difference between the two scenes can easily be explained. In the first scene the woman shamefully remained behind Jesus as if unworthy to approach him from in front. She is so lost in her grief that she does not care what the formal guests think about her. Her sole concern is how Jesus felt towards her. In the second scene Mary approaches Jesus from in front. With great stateliness she tries to captivate the attention of all, and focuses it on the dignity of the Messiah. Her desire is to extricate him from the danger of the religious leaders of the temple. Although the circumstances of both scenes are different, the techniques used seem to point towards the same woman. Nevertheless we cannot draw a conclusion merely on the similarity of attitudes.

Another significant fact, though also inconclusive, is that aside from the role of Jesus, John has practically made Mary Magdalene the heroine of his Gospel. He places her, as do the other evangelists, at the head of a group of women who faithfully follow Jesus through the dangers of his passion, his burial and his resurrection. John goes to great lengths to show that Mary is the *first* and *foremost* witness of the Risen Christ, as Mark 16, 9, explicitly states. Why, we ask ourselves, is such prominence given to a public sinner? John may have the answer.

Before proceeding with the lengthy story of "the Raising of Lazarus" in Chapter 11, John mentions the names of three persons of whom he had not yet spoken. "Lazarus," he says, "was from Bethany, the village of Mary and her sister Martha." With these words John refers us to the only other passage in the gospels (Lk. 10, 38-42), where mention is made of Mary and Martha of *Bethany*. Mary is sitting at the feet of Jesus, feeding her mind on his words of wisdom; while Martha, who is more concerned about material things, worries about the food of the body. Martha's aim is to involve her sister Mary in her own primary concern. By these few words we are well informed that all three persons are good friends of Jesus. Therefore it was quite natural for Mary and Martha to call on Jesus for assistance when their brother Lazarus had fallen into a serious sickness.

In the next sentence John wants to give us more information on this Mary who plays such an important role in his Gospel. He tells us that she is the same woman "who anointed the Lord with ointment and wiped his feet with her hair, whose brother Lazarus is ill." (11, 2.) In other words, John seems to tell us that previously it was Mary who was in trouble, and now it is her brother who needs help. The anointment mentioned in this passage cannot be the one of Bethany, about which John will only speak in Chapter 12. No writer tries to identify a person by referring to a future event. Moreover, John employs the past tense: Mary, who *had anointed* Jesus. Other than Luke's (7, 36-50) story of the public woman there is no account in all four Gospels of another woman having previously anointed Jesus' feet. Therefore we must necessarily conclude that John is referring to this particular event. John's second point of information to his readers is therefore that Mary of Bethany *is* the converted Public Woman as described by Luke.

Mary of Bethany Is Mary Magdalene (According to Jesus)

We have now brought the number of women down to two. The relationship of Mary of Bethany with regards to Mary Magdalene has yet to be examined. Mary of Bethany's real identity is revealed with absolute certainty by the one who knew Mary like a book, Jesus himself. As usual the particulars, lacking in the accounts of the synoptics, are supplied by John, who gives us the clue to the oral tradition existing before the time of the Gospels.

The place is Bethany, only a few miles outside of Jerusalem. It is now the fifth day before Good Friday and the sixth day before Passover. Simon the Leper holds a dinner for Jesus and his disciples who were on their way to celebrate the Passover in Jerusalem. Hospitality was customary, especially on this occasion. Lazarus was one of the many guests present at the feast. He too was a good friend of Simon. As usual Martha prepared the meal.

When everyone was seated, Mary, sister of Martha and Lazarus, made her appearance ... dressed in her best for the occasion, she attracted the attention of everyone present. However, she did not seek attention for herself, but wanted to bring the guests to realize the presence of the Messiah. She then lavishly poured a whole pound of the most expensive perfume on Christ's feet. Immediately the whole house was filled with this rare fragrance. The prodigality of Mary's act of love clashes sharply with the greed of Judas. Muttering angry remarks of disapproval, the miser tries to hide his love of money under the cover of sympathy for the poor. Three hundred pence worth of perfume have just slipped through his sticky fingers. Later on he would replace the loss with one-tenth of that sum, which was his reward for playing the traitor. (Jo. 12, 2-8.) Remove from this story all the names (except that of Simon the Leper) and most of the particulars. What remains is the account such as Mk. 14, 9, and Mt.

26, 6-13, had given to their readers, who were familiar with the background. To us, noncontemporaries, John supplied the key to the puzzle.

We continue our story where Jesus defends Mary against the avarice of Judas, as he had similarly defended her against the indignation of Martha and as he defended the public woman against the hypocrisy of Simon the Pharisee. "Why do you trouble the woman, when she has done me a last good deed? You will always be able to help the poor if you want to, but soon you will not be able to render me a service of this kind. Unknowingly this woman has anointed my body for burial." The undeniable impression which the reader gets from this last sentence is that this same woman, in keeping with the sacred Jewish tradition of the times, would soon try to embalm Christ's dead body, but to her great disappointment she would arrive too late to do so. Both Mark and Matthew have added Christ's words of defense to their stories of the Bethany anointing. Later on in their Gospels Mark and Luke will tell us how Mary Magdalene arrived with her spices on Easter morning, only to find that Jesus' body was no longer in the tomb. Jesus had given the magnanimous Mary the honor of his premature embalming.

Now follows the final and most momentous statement of Jesus. The introductory words "Truly I say to you" once more imply a statement of singular significance. "Wherever the gospel is preached in the whole world, what she has done, will be told in memory of her." (Mk. 14, 9; Mt. 26, 13.) Quite often commentators have passed over these words giving the vague and oversimplified explanation that Mary's name would become famous because her act of love would be publicly recorded wherever the Gospels would be read. However, Mark and Matthew have not even given the name of the woman who anointed Jesus in Bethany. Even if they had done so, however, we still would not understand the *intrinsic connection* between a simple act of love and the preaching of the Gospel.

Many persons have rendered acts of love to Jesus, and certainly not the least of all his mother Mary. Also Joanna, Mary of Clopas, Salome, Joseph of Arimathea and others were known for their exceptional services to Jesus. In none of these cases, however, did

Christ solemnly declare with the words, "Truly I say to you," that their acts of love would necessarily tie in with the main purpose of the Gospel. Perhaps if we compare the reason why God sent his Son to earth with the type of convert Mary Magdalene really was, we will have the answer to a riddle which seems worthy of being solved.

The Final Picture

Together with the exposition of Christ's doctrines, deeds and wonders the evangelists wanted to provide us with an outstanding example of the Gospel's primary objective. The reason for Jesus' coming on earth was to *search* for the Lost Sheep, or to seek out the weak sinner. It was useless to try to convert the self-righteous Pharisee who refused to admit the obvious fact of all his shortcomings. Of all the weak sinners, Mary Magdalene was just about as bad as anyone could get. Through the sincerity of her love, she rose from the lowest degree of selfishness to the highest degree of well-balanced love. As such, she would become a beacon of hope to weaklings of all generations. Wherever the Gospel would be preached, her story would be told as *the* most striking example of true conversion, a case where the worst sinner actually became the biggest saint. The reason for this spectacular conversion was "because she loved more."

The use of *contrasts* is an excellent method of expressing with clarity the things we really mean. Few modern writers have succeeded in using this method as efficiently as the evangelists have done. While the brigand Barabbas was set free in spite of his crimes, the innocent Jesus was crucified for no reason at all. While the ambitious apostles were arguing about who would be the boss, their real boss stood up and washed their feet. While the proud Pharisee was loudly proclaiming his own good deeds in the front of the temple, the humble taxpayer was confessing his failings in the rear of the building. Whereas Judas betrayed his Master for a mere thirty pieces of silver, Mary Magdalene tries to save Christ by spending ten times as much in value of perfume. Greed or selfish love turned the apostle-friend into a traitor. Unselfish love changed sinful Mary into a saint.

At the time the self-righteous Pharisees were greatly scandalized about Jesus' friendship with Mary Magdalene, Matthew, Zachaeus and others who admitted their mistakes. Even today for similar reasons, people are still reluctant to associate Mary Magdalene with the pious Mary of Bethany, or to identify the devout Mary with the public woman who converted in the house of Simon the Pharisee. The important thing in studying the Gospels is to look for the logic which the evangelists expressed with the symbols of their time. Mary left her home in Bethany, even as the prodigal son left his father's house. She also went to a distant country, which in her case was Magdala, where she led a life of total dissipation. As the father forgave his prodigal son, likewise Jesus forgave the repentant Mary. Although people would forever remember Mary's past by calling her the "Magdalene," Jesus would perpetuate her name and her conversion by making it the Gospel's outstanding example. All this happened because of Mary's superior quality of love. The one and only Mary would therefore be privileged to give Jesus a premature embalming, to be the first to witness his Resurrection, and to announce to Jesus' apostles, hiding for safety, the Good News of the "Risen Christ."

What better way was there for the Gospel writers to expose the need and power of forgiveness than to give a concrete example of what they really meant? Mary's conversion was a practical illustration of what Jesus' philosophy was all about and the proof that it actually worked. Confession or the admission of one's mistakes is nothing more than telling the truth to those who have the right to know since they have placed their trust in us. Everybody makes mistakes but not everybody is honest enough to keep his trustees informed. If superiors are entitled to an honest admission on the part of their subjects, then subjects have even more reason to demand the same from their superiors. After all a leader has no right to authority on the basis of his age and power but on the basis of his knowledge and his more edifying example.

Societies' leaders have much to learn in dealing with people. Their use of power and Pharisaic show have not made much of an impression on the on-coming generation. Young folks have sharp eyes that look beyond the screen of an artificial front. Leaders to them should be something more than a group of masqueraders. They seek guidance from people who know what they are doing and who do the thing for the purpose for which it was intended. Sly ways of doing things for secondary reasons are repulsive. If common sense demands that a law be broken, then a leader should be man enough to break the rule. The law is only a guideline. It consists of the spirit and the letter. When the letter is contrary to the spirit there is no reason for its application except to promote the spirit of hypocrisy. Blind obedience brings us back to the primitive period of social development. The seniors among the youths and the majority of the grown-ups today are far too well educated to return to the system of show and force. The unanswered question, "Are you for real or are you for show?" has incited the youth to launch a worldwide revolution against the fictitious set-up of our social structure.

Doing things for show can last for only a short while. After that the show becomes a flop because the important things have been neglected. Stimulating sincere concern for others is religion's primary function. Exposing self-interest without being offensive is religion's secondary role. The whole purpose of religion is therefore to give to society responsible leaders and conscientious citizens. By helping its members grow in honesty and dedication, by letting the people assume their own responsibility in matters of family and politics, by sticking to the rule of advising by word and example, religious leaders fulfill their mission and command the respect of their fellowmen. By losing sight of these spiritual functions, they ignore their mission and become contemptible in the eyes of their subjects.

Pharisaism is making religion consist in the blind observance of an ecclesiastical rule. A preliminary period of discipline is indispensable in teaching the need of order and self-control. Strict observance of the law has always been the first step by which a child or an unruly nation learns to respect the rights of others. Extending blind obedience unduly, however, is preventing a child from becoming an adult and a nation from developing into a democracy. Adult maturity means being able to impose discipline on one's self. One must be free from outside discipline in order to be able to impose discipline on one's self. A mature adult does not need to be forced by another person into doing that which is right. On the contrary, laws are often a hindrance in applying the right kind of help to one specific case. The handcuffs must therefore gradually be removed or a child will forever remain a child, a country a dictatorship, a prisoner a rebel. The Pharisee does not believe in removing handcuffs, even though the law defeats the purpose. He keeps people and their emotions in a state of underdevelopment.

Pharisaism does much more harm than sins of moral weakness. Human weakness is a form of neurosis, while Pharisaism is comparable to the final psychotic stage. The difference between neurosis and psychosis is often illustrated by humorous comparison. A neurotic, it is said, builds castles in the air. The psychotic lives in these castles, while the psychiatrist collects the rent. Obviously only an irresponsible psychiatrist would think of keeping his patients in their imaginary castles. The remainder of the saying is nevertheless quite true.

Psychosis is a higher degree and the permanent form of neurosis. Neurosis is everybody's illness, however slight it be. Letting our emotions over-run our thinking is undoubtedly a neurotic trend. Drives and emotions occasionally get the upper hand, no matter how much self-control we claim to possess. Outside of Jesus, no one has ever had perfect control over all of his emotions. When emotions take over to the point that we are unable to curb them, bad habits can no longer be identified as a weakness but a permanent fixture. Selfish love has then become an accepted condition and a fixed idea similar to the Pharisee's blind adherence to the law. Those who freeze their feelings for deserving needs of humanity, because they are afraid of opposing the law, lose their normal feelings and attitude towards people. The repression of rational feelings destroys natural feelings and produces those sentiments which are unnatural and abnormal.

The Pharisee keeps his mind and feelings like the body of a dwarf, in the impossibility of being able to develop to full growth. Both the weak sinner and the Pharisee indulge in selfish love, the one in a moment of blind passion, the other with the malice of premeditation. Refusing to help where help is needed is just as selfish as indulging in unwarranted pleasures. The one does it when his mind is in the fog. The other does it when his mind is in the clear. The one has a weak will while the other has a bad will. Hiding forever behind the shell of ceremonial rituals and closing one's eyes to the real needs of people is without the least bit of doubt the attitude of a mental patient.

If controlling neurotic tendencies is everybody's full-time job, then falling short is everybody's constant weakness. In other words we are all in a constant state of fluctuation between emotions and reasons, between sin and justification, between prejudice and impartiality. The object of living is to learn the difficult task of directing our love and feelings intelligently. Sometimes we are successful, other times we are not. At times our ignorance is pardonable, at times it is inexcusable. Some people are willing to admit their mistakes but the Pharisees and the hardened sinners have no such intentions. Of the three categories of sinners, curiously enough, only the weak sinner is the one to be considered as a balanced individual. He alone is in contact with reality because he admits the facts of his irrational behavior. His irrational conduct and disregard of others disturb his inner peace and happiness. Unlike the two others, he is not looking for an alibi. The hardened sinner is just the opposite. He has given up the struggle and made peace with the enemy. Because he justifies the irrational, he is out of contact with reality. Getting him to accept a situation as it actually exists is the difficult job of a psychologist who puts stock in the reward of the hereafter.

Although there's still hope for the hardened sinner with a crippling habit, the condition of the Pharisee is next to impossible. No one can convince the Pharisee that every law is tied up with innumerable cases which do not apply. A hardened sinner justifies his irrational conduct because his habits have become over-powering. A Pharisee justifies the law enforcement because his stubbornness is stronger then his use of reason. The one is morally unable to shake his bad habit. The other is mentally unwilling to drop his blindness. The first man needs help. The second man does not want help or change. Christ forgave the weak sinners, he cured the addicts and evil-possessed, but he resisted the unwilling fanatics. The Pharisee is out of contact with reality, not because his habits are over-powering, but because he has lost his natural feelings for the real needs of his fellowmen. As far as he is concerned the law is always holy, even when it kills and very often that is exactly what it does.

Mary Magdalene was an example of a hardened sinner. The Master Physician helped her out of her chronic sickness of selfish love. Unlike psychologists who do not believe in the hereafter, Christ knew how to bring lost souls back to reality and to make them want to be genuinely helpful to others. His specialty was to turn sinners into leaders. Most of his leaders were weak sinners. Many of them were hardened sinners. Some of them were even Pharisees, such as Nicodemus, Joseph of Arimathea and Paul, the apostle of the gentiles.

Of necessity Pharisaism will always be religion's foremost enemy. Does not religion depend on discipline for its first push to get off to a good start? Mature religion is based on self-discipline, but before you can discipline yourself, you must first learn to respect the rights of others in a disciplinary setting. People make self-discipline their way of life, if the discipline which they have received has been fair and just. Discipline leads to self-discipline, when it has been applied correctly. Past discipline that has been unfair or extended beyond the period of inexperience brings on resentment because it is more of a hindrance than a means of help. Christ did away with the disciplinary approach to religion except of course for those who do not know what the rights of others are all about. The inexperienced youth will always have to be set straight by those who take their conduct to heart.

The religious-minded have always been tempted to use force in the attempt to do away with evil. The difficulty with forcing religion onto others is that everyone has the God-given right of directing himself. Evil is an act of our free will, by which we seek personal advantage where it does not make sense to do so. Evil consists in pursuing our own interests regardless of other peoples' rights. Young people may be restrained by those who are responsible for teaching the rational way of living. Sooner or later, however, the push must stop in order to make way for adult responsibility. The leader's example and the rationality of unselfish love must replace the preliminary period of force. If this does not happen, discipline will not have served its purpose. A mother must let go the hand of her child if she wants her child to learn how to walk by itself.

Sinful love is often better than no love at all. As long as we keep on trying, there still is hope that our love will one day become unselfish. The gunner who misses the target has a better chance in becoming a marksman than the man who does not as much as give it a try. Selfish love of the past can be undone, provided we do not enclose ourselves within the walls of self-righteousness. The Pharisee has locked himself within an impregnable fortress of legal rationalization. Yet his justice is as hollow as his heart is void of feeling. Instead of examining himself, which is his foremost responsibility, he spends all his time in unkind and unfair judgements. By adhering blindly to the mechanism of a legal system he fails to see the real needs of people and what is worse he ends up by not even caring. Having fallen into the habit of judging others purely on the basis of legal adherence, he is as blind as a bat. Instead of examining himself he spends his time in criticizing others. What a pitiful way for a leader to be. No wonder the youth has rebelled against the emptiness of such undesirable impostors. Surely Christ did not want his leaders to fall into the miserable trap of becoming a piece of machinery. We have seen how selfish love can be transformed into a soothing ointment of helpful love. Perhaps forceful direction can undergo a similar change. Everyone can become a leader of love, if he is courageous enough to overcome his selfish ambitions. Jesus has shown us the qualities of good leadership. In the next chapter we will see if his immediate disciples have benefited from what they have learned in their school.

Chapter VI

THE LEADERSHIP OF LOVE

Human love is meant for people. The social element of loving people is the first requirement of well-balanced love. The second is that we love others as much as ourselves. There is nothing wrong in loving ourselves in the first place, provided our love retains the proper proportions. Still, love will never make us happy unless it includes the needs of other people as well as our own. "Whoever drinks of the water which I shall give him will never thirst." (Jo. 4, 14.) Human love is designed for people. People should love people, not animals or things. The reason for animals and things is to help us improve our love for those of our kind. If we isolate ourselves like a hermit or have more feelings for animals and things than for people, love runs into a psychological derailment. If we love people for personal advantage, love is a make-believe for altruistic interest. If we love people in proportion to their needs without expecting a personal bonus, love is what it was meant to be. What all this adds up to is that, outside of our measure of unselfish love all other distinctions of rank and power among people are of secondary importance. No matter what nationality, creed or race, people are members of one large family. It is our job to direct love in proportion to the need of the individual. Whether we want to admit it or not we really are our brother's own keeper.

Though unselfish dedication would make of this world a heavenly utopia, such love can hardly be spelled out by rule or regulation. Society cannot force people to render service where service is needed. Everyone is free to establish his own measure of usefulness. Besides, all the geniuses in the world could not compose a law which is not subject to innumerable exceptions and interpretations. All society can do is to give certain general directives that must be applied with common sense and punish the man who infringes upon the rights of another.

The harder people fight for personal interest, the less scrupulous will they be in depriving others of their rights. The result is that more and more laws have to be made to counteract the injustice that has been done. After this vicious circle has gone on long enough, legislation will finally succumb on account of its overload of technicalities. Because selfish love will have done away with the use of common sense, excessive restrictions will have done away with the possibility of living in society. The youth all over the world is breaking away from stuffy social structure. They are forming societies of their own and not necessarily better ones. The cold war between law and circumvention of the law is now at a peak. Covered hostility is not only a phenomenon that occurs between countries of opposing ideologies. It can develop between the government and citizens of the same nation.

Cold war does exist between the leadership and subjects of our own country as well as it exists between the capitalistic and communistic countries of the world. Socialism and communism have tried to establish equality between citizens. They have failed because they have misunderstood the basic element of human love. Human love is free insofar as it cannot be prescribed. It is everyone's privilege to direct his love any way he chooses. Religious institutions have made the usual mistake of pressuring their subjects by forcing them to take the vows. The most fundamental rule of psychology is that grown-ups must be treated as individuals. Constant liberty to make one's own decision is what allows a person to be himself. "Let your 'yes' be a 'yes' and your 'no' a 'no.' "

If love and social equality cannot be imposed, if social living is an absolute necessity, how then can society enjoy the tranquility of peace and order? The answer is by introducing the right kind of leadership in social direction. Forceful leadership must be the exception. Exemplary leadership must be the general rule. Leaders who stand behind the right answer, instead of hiding behind the dignity of their title, are leaders who win their subjects' esteem. Leaders who use authority for their own selfish purposes are leaders who are breeding contempt for their use of power. The whole concept of leadership is to give to the less experienced the correct answer and example. If the inexperienced are disgruntled by the leadership of those who are experienced, then the inexperienced will obviously be searching for leadership among their own kind. Being inexperienced themselves they will eventually be listening to the desires of flesh, as St. Paul puts it. (2 Tim. 4, 3.)

Why do students need a teacher if not to explain to them the scientifically proven facts? Why do children need parents except to learn the real sense of responsibility? Why do all leaders need spiritual leaders except to remind them of the behavioral principles of their own rational nature? Was this not what Christ's teaching to his disciples was all about? IF THE WORLD IS IN A CHAOS TODAY IT IS SIMPLY BECAUSE LEADERS ARE NOT GOOD LEADERS. A poor leader's interest lies within himself. You cannot blame the youth for rebelling against an authority whose mind is made up ahead of time and who refuses to discuss the advantages of a change. Such stubborn authority does not even care about finding the right solution to a problem. It pretends to know the answers without proof or test.

The time for blind trust and obedience is when the mind is at a stage of insufficient development or disturbed because of a previous nervous breakdown. After that comes the period of intelligent and responsible leadership. Christ did not call his adult followers to be blind thinkers but to use their God-given brains in a way which makes sense. Follow a blind leader blindly he says and you will be well on your way to finding yourself in a ditch. The reason for following a leader is because what he says and does makes sense. The reason for not following a leader is because what he says and does makes no sense or is nonsense. Reason is then the ultimate foundation of all authority, even that of the Bible. If such be the case, leadership had better show a little more interest in constructive suggestions or forever hold its peace. Putting on a grandiose show to gain popularity or flattering the people of the opposition is a deceitful way of trying to win favor. Show-off leaders are not seriously interested in helping others where serious help is needed.

They are much too busy working at their personal success. A good leader does not have to use bribery, flattery or ostentation to win a vote of confidence. Public office has nothing to offer to a person who merely wants to serve.

Humanly speaking, good leadership is far from being an easy task or a pleasurable position. The ability to solve social problems is only a preliminary requirement. The ability to inspire others by personal conviction is leadership's most important trait. Good leadership requires a great deal of unselfish love along with an unlimited amount of dedication. No one can be a leader for glory and self-interest and still be a good one. By far the greatest number of well-known leaders were out for personal fame. Lenin, Napoleon and Hitler were all big leaders at the expense of the lives of others. A good leader is not one who takes lives but one who is ready to give his own for the good of the sheep, after the example of the Good Shepherd. Religious, civil and parental hirelings are responsible for the disorders which have turned the world into a bloody arena. Good leadership is the thing the world needs most of all, more than food, more than health, jobs or money. "The harvest is plentiful but the labors are few. Pray therefore the Lord of the harvest to send laborers (good leaders) into his harvest." (Mt. 9, 37-38.) What the world lacks most is more of "the right men in the right place." Unselfish leaders leave a greater and more lasting effect on society. Doctor Albert Schweitzer, Abraham Lincoln, Doctor Livingston, Mahatma Gandhi and others were all great and good leaders and yet the leadership of Jesus has overshadowed them all. It might be interesting to know how well Christ's personally trained leaders succeeded in the most challenging field of human achievements.

When for the first time in history, a large number of Catholic theologians in America questioned both the extent of the Pope's authority and his personal infallibility, the scriptural texts which were cited in support of these views had to be reexamined and confronted with the logic of Jesus. This we have done in part III of Chapter IV. In the course of the present chapter we would like to check on the actual use which the apostles have made of their prerogatives. The whole problem of religious leadership can be summed up with the simple question of whether early Christian rule was monarchical or democratic. As we recall, the Eastern Orthodox schism of the eleventh century was mainly caused by the monarchical claims of Rome. Later on, the Protestant separation of the sixteenth century was introduced for much the same reason. There is little doubt that the Apostles, who were trained by the Master and had given their lives for his ideals, did not deviate from the authentic standards of leadership which Christ had laid down. The story of their calling, appointment and early ministry will hopefully shed some light on the correct form of early Christian leadership.

Background and Calling of the Twelve

The fourth evangelist, 1, 29, tells us that after Jesus had prepared himself for his public ministry by forty days of fasting, prayer and temptations, he left the desert and came to Bethany on the east side of the Jordan, the place where John ordinarily performed his baptisms. Christ's intentions were to look for future leaders from among those whom the Baptist had already prepared. As Jesus was passing by, John pointed him out to his own followers by saying, "Behold the Lamb of God who takes away the sins of the world." (Jo. 1, 29.) On the next day Jesus again walked by the same area. This time John beckoned Andrew and another disciple to go up to the Messiah and get acquainted. The anonymous "other disciple" was most probably no one else than John the Evangelist himself, describing his first encounter with Jesus. He betrays himself with the knowledge of minute detail. He met Jesus for the first time at 4 P.M., a moment never-to-be-forgotten. (Jo. 1, 39.) These two men spent the evening at Jesus' residence. Andrew was so deeply impressed with his visit that the very next day he brought his brother Simon along. Upon seeing Simon for the first time, Jesus said, "You are Simon, son of John. You will be called Cephas which means Peter" (a rock). (Jo. 1, 41.)

On the fourth day of his public ministry, Jesus sees Philip, who also was anxious to meet the Emmanuel. Philip, like Andrew, had been so captivated by the personality of Jesus that he coaxed his distrustful friend Nathanael into coming along. Nathanael is generally taken to be Bartholomew or son of Tolmai. Philip was from Bethsaida, the city of Andrew and Peter. (Jo. 1, 44.) Mark 1, 21, states however, that Peter and Andrew were from Capernaum, also a fishing town on the northwest bank of the Galilean Sea. This little village was the home of Peter's mother-in-law. It is quite possible that Peter was originally from Bethsaida as John the Evangelist indicates. After his marriage he no doubt lived with his mother-in-law at Capernaum. Leaving Nazareth, Jesus made his new abode in the same village, probably in the same house. (Mk. 2, 1.) We read that when Jesus had cured Peter's mother-in-law, "she served them." (Mk. 1, 31b.) Judging by the fact that this woman was still alive and that Peter's death only took place during the Neronian persecution about 65 A.D., which was 36 years later, Peter at this time was not an old man, as he is frequently shown to be in paintings. Very probably Peter was then in his early thirties.

Mark 1, 16f, describes a few subsequent meetings of Jesus with his disciples on the Galilean shore near Capernaum. Jesus had invited Simon and Andrew, and shortly thereafter James and John, the sons of Zebedee, to leave their nets and become fishers of men. Matthew in 9, 9 tells us how he made Jesus' acquaintance. He is Levi, the tax-collector, son of Alpheus. (Mk. 2, 14.) The individual contacts which Jesus had made with the rest of the apostles previous to their final assignment as tribe-leaders of his new kingdom are not recorded. However, the later appointment of the TWELVE as they were first called (before the technical name of "apostles" was coined) is solemnly announced by all three synoptics. (Mt. 10, 2; Mk. 3, 13f; Lk. 6, 12f.) Mark says that Jesus had spent the night in prayer. The next morning he selected from a vast number of disciples, as many leaders for his new kingdom as there were tribal heads in Israel. Everyone will recall that Jacob or Israel had twelve sons who became the leaders of the Jewish nation.

The limited details of Jesus' encounter with his future leaders brings out a very interesting point. All the apostles were impatiently awaiting the coming of God's personal Representative. Consequently they needed very little encouragement to become his disciples as soon as they knew the truth about his identity. In fact, they were so anxious to meet the Messiah that great distances did not frighten them. The distance from Capernaum to Bethany is about ninety miles. Family cares and the job of earning a living had to fit in with the work of helping to establish the new spiritual kingdom. Their primary aim was to get the people to accept God as the boss of their lives. Whether leaders or not, all Christians were expected to place spiritual concerns above earthly considerations. "Whoever loves his father or mother . . . son or daughter more than me, is not worthy of me" (Mt. 10, 37,) "and whoever shall do the will of my Father who is in heaven, he is my brother and sister and mother." (Mt. 12, 50.)

The difference between what is required on the part of a leader and on the part of a non-leader or layman is only a matter of degree. Aside from spending most of their time in the task of spreading the good news, leaders were expected to sell their property and lay the proceeds of what was sold at the feet of the apostles. The community money was then distributed according to the degree of every person's needs. (Acts 4, 34-35.) The reason why Ananias and his wife were struck dead at Peter's feet was that they wanted to be leaders, but refused to pay the price. They did not fully trust God's providence for the needs of the body. Consequently they procured themselves a worldly form of security by hanging on to a part of their money. Here we have too much dependency on worldly means and not enough dependency on the power of faith. (Acts 5, 2.) The rich man who was asked to sell his belongings and give the money to the poor was also unfit to show others the way. Money meant more to him than trying to help people towards a charitable disposition. (Mk. 10, 17s.) The man who wanted to bury his father before joining Christ on his missionary tours lacked unselfish love in a different way. He placed family affairs above the need of spreading God's kingdom. (Mt. 8, 21.)

We read that the apostles who had left their nets in order to follow Jesus went back to fishing in order to support themselves and their families. Yet the establishment of God's kingdom on earth had become their primary occupation. Furthermore, most of the apostles including Peter and the brothers of the Lord were married and took their wives with them on their missionary trips. (1 Cor. 9, 5.) Paul and John appear to be the exceptions. Celibacy is therefore not absolutely necessary to lead others to God. Although he who is able to make himself a eunuch for the sake of the kingdom of heaven has certain advantages over a man with family responsibilities, still every leader must judge which is best for himself, to get married or to remain single. (1 Cor. 7, 9 and 34.) The single minister is able to give his undivided attention to the needs of his flock.

Their Assignment and Mission as Leaders

During his own life, Jesus was the one who decided whether a candidate had sufficient faith and detachment to qualify as a leader of religion. On these two things depend largely whether a candidate has a real vocation or not. Then wishing to teach future church leaders to make their choice of successors depend on virtue and not on know-how or favoritism, he prayed all night before making a decision himself. After commissioning the Twelve leaders of God's earthly kingdom, he ordered them to go forth and remind the people to live by their conscience. First he sent his disciples to the lost sheep (sincere sinners) of the house of Israel. (Mt. 10, 5.) After his Resurrection, he told them to extend their message to all the nations of the world. (Mt. 28, 19.)

Christ's message was simple and to the point. God had sent his personal Representative to earth because he loved all peoples and wanted to give them a perfect example of rational human behavior. By imitating Christ's way of living and by following his common sense advice, the people would earn their eternal salvation. By salvation is meant that God would make all good men rise gloriously, just as he had raised his favorite Son. (Acts, 10, 40.) Salvation is the reward which comes to us from God, because God alone can raise the human body and transform it into a glorified entity. Salvation is indirectly the work of man, because it depends on us to make ourselves worthy of a glorious resurrection. Salvation is also the work of Jesus, because Jesus is the one who showed us the way and told us what to do.

In view of these facts, the apostles called themselves the preachers of the "Risen Christ." They told the people everything which they had seen and heard. Jesus of Nazareth had been strung on the cross because he had taken a firm stand against the bigotry and corruption of his time. His strongest opposition came from the religious leaders who by profession should have been the outstanding example of unbias. In spite of their resistance, God had made his Son conquer the violence of his evil-minded opponents. Those who wished to repent from their own wrong-doings must band together in a close-knit brotherhood of unselfish dedication. By accepting to be baptized in public, candidates pledged their fidelity to each other and to the cause which they held in common. During their regular meetings they checked on themselves by the commemoration of "the Lord's supper." Basically this means that they revived their spirit of fellowship by examining their conscience, by reading passages of Scripture, by renewing their promises and by a common recital of songs and prayers. Those who persevere in the practice of pure altruistic love to which they have committed themselves can expect the same glorious resurrection which God had given to his Son. The glorification of the body, however, will only take place at the end of the world. At that crucial moment God will send his Son once more to us. Jesus' second coming will no longer be within the framework of compassion and forgiveness but in the light of a judge who knows no pity. When this tremendous moment of "the Day of the Lord" will take place nobody knows. God has not even confided this secret to his own beloved Son. Besides eternal happiness there is also an earthly reward for imitating Jesus in "the cause for truth and right." A hundredfold or an unlimited amount of peace will come to the man who lives by his conscience. (Acts 2, 38-42; Jo. 5, 28-29; 1 Cor. 15, 12-15; Mt. 24, 36; Mt. 19, 29.)

Such was the message which the disciples had to bring from house to house. If the residents of these homes had not lost all sense of responsibility, they would be thrilled with the Good News of peace and happiness. In return, they would gladly take care of the messengers' bodily needs. Should the sinners, however, refuse to listen to these words of comfort, then the Apostles were told to leave that house and shake the dust from their feet. This gesture was a sign that the sinner was unworthy of God's mercy. (Mt. 10, 10-14.)

As is evident by these words, the primary goal of apostolic preaching was to cure the individual's egotistical ways, which bring about friction in a conglomeration of people. Only secondarily were the apostles to remedy the *effects* of selfish love, such as hunger, conflicts, illness and others. Selfish love is caring too much for one's self or for the needs of lesser importance. Such love is sinful or irrational because all people have needs which have to be fulfilled and all human needs are not all on one and the same level. In moral terminology, irrational love has been given the name of sin. Selfish living apparently leads to death and destruction, or as Saint Paul put it, "the wages of sin is death." (Rom. 6, 23.)

Sin is man's animalistic tendency of "the survival of the fittest" colliding with the superior demands of our sense of proportions. We could define sin as a deliberate and irrational deed of selfish love making social living a complete impossibility. Usually such deeds deprive other people of what is rightfully theirs. Earthquakes and hurricanes may bring about woes. Such afflictions can hardly compare with the woes caused by the bad will of people. In the case of the man born blind (Jo. 9, 1-3.) it so happened that this man's blindness was not caused by his own immoral living nor by that of his parents. Yet behind the fact that nature is the cause of certain pains, trials and of death beyond our control, there lies also the fact that WE are more frequently the cause of worse or similar harm. In one word all of us have sinned.

In prevision of this fact and also to make us earn our reward, God placed us here on earth, as it were, in a paradise which we lost by selfish living. "Just as through one man's sin (Adam's, denoting mankind) condemnation came unto all of mankind, so also through one man's righteousness (Christ's meaning Christianity) the justification of life came to us all." (Rom. 5, 18.)

In the beginning of Christianity the apostles, few in number, were engrossed with the spreading of God's word or with trying to get the people to be good to each other. They were endowed with exceptional charismatic gifts, by which they could soften the hardened hearts of obstinate sinners. Sometimes they were even known to make physical ailments disappear. However, they had neither time nor means to get personally involved in the field of charity. That is why they asked their faithful to pick out seven men of repute, filled with the Spirit of wisdom, to tend to the distribution of food. (Acts 6, 1-6.)

The word of God and the works of charity are actually as closely related to each other as sin is the usual cause of pains and of heartaches. Preaching the word of God is explaining the theory of unselfish love. Doing charity is putting this theory into practice. The one goes with the other as cause and effect. The apostles had lay committees tend to the parishioners' temporary needs. Our modern parishes have a long way to go in getting the laity actively involved in the corporal and spiritual works of mercy or the needs of their people. Most parishes are interested only in raising money for the glory of the institution. They are doing the direct opposite of what the Gospel recommends for them to do. If parishes are going to survive the revolutionary pressure of an unhappy community, they had better stop using their ministry as a means of enriching their "institution." Real Christianity is generally found among the poor instead of the rich. Only false leaders spend their time with the affluent and the influential.

After the death of the apostles, extraordinary charismatic gifts were almost a thing of the past.* Religious leaders now had to depend exclusively on their personal faith and charity to win the confidence of their people. When the faithful detect in their pastor a deep concern for people in distress, pastoral support will never be a problem. Church leaders who rely on a clever financial system for raising money and who embarrass their people with publicized lists

---

* Virtuous living, complete detachment and readiness to suffer were the basic qualities of most Christians as long as the heat of the Roman persecutions was on. Just as the sensible interpretation of musical compositions depends on the previous mastery of the techniques of music (scales, beat, exercises etc.) so also the correct use of the gifts of tongues, pentecostalism etc. depends on our previous mastery of religion's fundamentals. Virtuosity follows the mastery of the techniques.

of contributions, intentionally ignore Jesus' advice when he said, "Let not your left hand know what your right hand is doing." (Mt. 6, 3.) Religion which is run like a business, instead of being borne by the principles of faith, is nothing more than a business using religion as a cover-up. Where people have lost confidence in their leaders and interest in their sermons on account of their lucrative goals, it may be advisable to stop preaching altogether and simply return to the practice of charity. In this way there is a possibility that people will slowly regain trust in the words of their leaders. Jesus gave the same advice to the poor leaders of his time, when he told them to make friends for themselves by means of the mammon of iniquity. (Lk. 16, 9.) The good-Samaritan approach will always remain effective where all other methods have been known to be useless.

The apostles had given up their rights to personal property. The buildings which they used, such as the headquarters of the church of Jerusalem, of Antioch, etc., belonged to a member of their congregation. Eventually, when the church was officially recognized by the state, they became the property of the church. All leaders were instructed to sell all that they possessed and place the proceeds in the hands of a bursar. When Jesus was still alive Judas was the bursar of the Twelve. The elders of the churches sent their men out on the road, instead of waiting for the people to come to them. While on the road, they were not allowed to take food and money with them and were permitted only a single set of clothing. (Mk. 6, 8.)

If the church authorities of today were to forbid their leaders the right to personal property, the leaders would either circumvent the ruling or quit their jobs. Times and social conditions have undergone such fundamental changes that detachment of material things must necessarily be on a voluntary basis. In certain extraordinary circumstances, such as in missions, in homes or in charitable institutions, volunteers may yet be found, generous enough, to share their goods with those of their co-workers. The sharing would then be of course on a strictly voluntary basis. Community property works fine in marriage, so why could it not exist where people spontaneously agree to pool their goods for the accomplishment of a charitable enterprise? In general, however, conditions favorable to community property in an affluent and freedom-loving society are more or less a thing of the past even among the Mennonites.

When Christ advised his leaders to pool their property, he wanted them to depend on faith for their support, instead of being materialistically minded and enjoying absolute security. As proof of their faith, they had to give up their possessions and live on the charity of their followers. A guaranteed income is not living on faith and on charity. A good leader will want to keep himself poor instead of giving the impression of being poor by living under a circumvented vow of poverty. All church leaders should therefore be recognized by their love of poverty, whether their property be personal or owned by the church. Nothing does more harm to religion than to see its leaders turn to real estate, gluttony and mundane living.

There were times when the apostles had no friends or homes to turn to neither for food nor for shelter. Saint Paul tells us how he worked at tents with Aquilla, an Italian Jew in Corinth, in order to earn his living. (Acts 18, 1-3.) The life and feelings of a true Christian leader are touchingly expressed in Saint Paul's farewell speech to the elders of Ephesus. "You yourselves know," he says, "that these hands have ministered to my necessities and to the needs of those who stayed with me." (Acts 20, 34.) Although a spiritual leader is entitled to have a family and receive support from his congregation, Saint Paul never took advantage of these privileges. The opposite extreme of taking too much advantage of the faithful's support is when clergymen spend most of their time in earning their own living or in holding down a secular job. In choosing laborers for the work of his vineyard Christ expected his leaders to spend most of their time in becoming fishermen of men."

In France several priests wanting to identify with the working class have become workers themselves. Also in our country and abroad, some of the newly ordained clergymen are reluctant to accept the traditional job of curates. Instead of parish-work, they are looking for a ministry by which they can become one with the youth. Living under a pastor who runs the parish like a business and keeps lucrative superstition alive is not exactly the dream of a young man who is trying to live up to religious idealism. Most parishes have lost practically all of their youth. The young clergy wish to re-establish contact with those whom the parish system has thoroughly disgusted. Building up understanding with the future generation is certainly an excellent idea, as long as the religious leader is truly a leader and also a good one. Sometimes it's the other way around, nl., that the leader is the one who is led by his followers.

To lead people who want logical answers, one has to be able to solve their problems in a satisfactory fashion. It so happens that the philosophy of rational human behavior is the main specialty of the Bible, that is, if one digs deep enough for logical answers and looks for the lesson of rational human behavior. The religious leader who does not look for answers in the Bible is like a shoemaker who does not believe in sticking to his last. You do not go to a doctor when there is something wrong with the motor of your car, unless your doctor is at the same time a specialist in mechanics. If, in a backward area, fixing cars makes the sick drop their belief in witchcraft and look for the scientifically proven medical care, a doctor will not have wasted his time by tinkering with mechanics. There is always the danger, however, that the doctor-mechanic may lose the idealism of his profession.

Too much freedom in the exercise of ministry is as bad as no latitude at all. Laws determining the field of ministry should be sufficiently flexible so as not to preclude a personal adaptation of help to the spiritual needs of the times. As to the traditional form of parochial ministry, much trouble could be avoided if parishes were organized after the original pattern of the apostolic times. Saint Paul placed all his churches under a group of exemplary leaders just as soon as the church was able to function on its own.

In the selection of church leaders the apostles looked for un-equivocal signs of good character rather than for intellectual or administrative qualities. (Acts 13, 15; 16, 25.) They had in mind the good of the sheep and not the glory of the institution. Consequently the leaders were not expected to give blind obedience to rules but intelligent care to the needs of the flock. Just as a good tree bears good fruit so it is with the religious churches in a selection of leaders and members. The qualifications which were essential to religion in early times are just as essential to the religion of today. Failure to look for these characteristics in the selection of members will soon turn a church into a group of pretenders. Every church member should be known for his integrity, sincerity and serviceability. The past poor religious leadership was guilty of running after the rich and the education of their children. The present poor religious leadership is guilty of giving new members a brainwashing indoctrination. In early Christian times catechumens had to undergo a trial period of Christian living based on the study of the Bible and the imitation of Christ. After satisfactory probation of conduct the elders would vote on the retention or rejection of the candidate. If democratic vote was already necessary in the early stages of Christianity, then it is more so at our advanced age of culture.

Their Power

We have followed the Twelve from their lowly position as fishermen up to their noble appointment as founders of the spiritual kingdom. We must now follow them in the exercise of that power by which they kept their organization alive. Much as a group of people may believe in the life of the hereafter, some form of earthly power is still necessary to prevent the evil minded from disrupting the unity of mind and heart among the members. Christ had toppled the O.T. hierarchy of high priests, Sanhedrin members (seventy), and temple priests. He replaced the Mosaic and Pharasaic "Do nots" by a single commandment of "Do" unto others as you would have others to do unto you. He denounced the stuffy leadership of the Scribes and Sadducees with their crippling methods of fear. He changed the primitive form of a compulsory religion into a religion where love is self-directed.

The faithful would no longer have to give blind obedience to the prescriptions of an institution. Their obedience would now have to meet the demands of common sense. God gave man reason to enable him to direct himself intelligently. The new leaders were not to burden their followers with numerous directives. Christian leaders must learn to lead without coercive methods. They must lead with love, service and example. The whole community, leaders and all, were to be led by the spirit and not by inflexible rules. No single person must lord it over another.

113

Great as this rational direction of love may sound, it still was necessary to give leaders some sort of power in preventing the deceptive wolf in sheepskin from destroying the flock. Jesus was extremely careful not to let power fall into the hands of a single individual. Only the church leaders as a group were allowed to decide over the expulsion of someone who was accused of misbehavior. (Mat. 18, 17b.)

Excommunication is a very dangerous weapon when in the hands of one single individual. Autocrats use power to make others comply with their personal wishes. Excommunication was not intended to make one person afraid of another but to make every person afraid of losing his friends. Through the conscious voice of reason God makes his will known to people. To distinguish God's voice from our own wishful thinking or worse from our falling into the condition of hearing voices, we must have sufficient candor to let the people express their honest opinions and not place unfair restrictions on the freedom of the press. Science and common sense are sufficiently powerful to handle the rest.

God wants us to think objectively and stick to reality by the mere fact that He gave us the ability of sensitive and intelligent perception. Objective adherence to the conditions of reality is therefore the sum total of everything that Christ came to tell us. The basics of Christianity are necessarily self-evident and indisputable principles of common sense. The spiritual leader who uses the gentile method of force must make sure that he is not using it merely as a personal weapon for political ends. His decision will be God's will and not his own if, besides adhering to a collective judgment, he also keeps an open mind. Most individuals do not when given full power over the fate of another. That is why Jesus made only a promise to Peter at the occasion of the latter's solemn profession of faith: "I *will* give you the keys to the kingdom of heaven." (Mt. 16, 19.)

The actual bestowal of the power of excommunication was therefore not given to Peter alone, but to the whole group of elders united in a body. Matthew places it after the case of the man who, having given public offense, had ignored fraternal correction and even the warning of the entire group of church leaders. "If he does not listen to the *church* let him be to you as a gentile or tax-

114

collector." (Mt. 18, 17b.) Whereupon Matthew goes on to say, "truly I say to *you* whatever you bind on earth shall be bound in heaven, and whatever you loose on earth shall be loosed in heaven." (Mt. 18, 18.) The words *church* and *you* are therefore one and the same thing, namely, the apostles combined in one solid group. (See Chapter IV part III).

To make it even more clear that no single person has the right "to lord it over another," Matthew starts Chapter 18 off with the contention among the disciples about which one of them would be the greatest. Which one of the Twelve would have the right to make the others comply with his wishes?* The same dispute would come up again, when James and John, the sons of Zebedee wanted to make up a triumvirate rule for the new kingdom and sit on either side of Jesus. (Mk. 10, 37.) The mere fact that this dispute is described five times should be enough to make a person with average intelligence sit up and take notice.

Rule or leadership can be maintained either by using power or merely by setting the right kind of example. Christ calls the first form of leadership "the gentile way of ruling." (Mk. 10, 42.) He opposes the "power-rule" to his "Christian-rule" by example, whereby no power is used but only a greater amount of service and love. Then Jesus tells his followers, if after a sincere effort has been made to save the scandal-giver, it appears necessary to use the gentile rule to protect innocent children or the community from bad example, then this power must be used by the church leaders collectively; "Whatever you bind on earth . . . " (Mt. 18, 18.) After the bestowal of community power follows the commendation of community prayer: "If two or more are gathered in my name, there am I in the midst of them." (Mt. 18, 19-20.) The principle behind this artless description is that the whole Christian community must be led by God's spirit, by the majority vote of those who go to God to remain objective in their thinking. All decisions must come from the community as a whole or from its elders who rely on God's help in

---

* See parallel texts: Mk. 9, 33-35, and Lk. 9, 46-47. Also Lk. 22, 24.

arriving at a realistic solution.

The Pre-eminence of Peter

If no single individual is an exclusive holder of power, what then happens to Peter's position as head of the church? Did not Jesus pick Simon out from among the others and tell him to feed his lambs and feed his sheep? Were not the keys promised to Peter alone and passed over in silence at the moment of the bestowal of power to the apostolic group? Is not Peter the constant spokesman of the Twelve and is he not always mentioned first in the listings of the apostles? No one can deny that Peter enjoyed a pre-eminence over the rest of the apostles. Jesus conferred on him a spiritual paternity which did not give the others cause for feelings of resentment. Peter had more courage than the others and was always the first to tackle a job. Ambitious at first, he finally understood that a good leader was only a bigger servant. He learned to carry out the wishes of the majority instead of making the majority carry out his own desires. In a truly spiritual community no one sticks out above the other, except the one who has gradually worked himself into becoming a more useful servant. Rank should be a non-existent thing. When everyone is competing with his neighbor in trying to give better service, then truly the humblest servant is the best man in the crowd.

The father-image is as necessary in the fold of Christianity as it is in a family and in the human race at large. All members of the family look up to their father for examples of wisdom, of courage and of goodness. To him they listen not so much because they are pushed but because they are drawn. Although all the members of the family take part in a family decision, the father generally has the right answers to everyone's problems or cares enough to find them. As Robert Young's T.V. program has it "father knows best."

To apply the Christian principles of leadership to the structures of the church, each local Christian community should make its humblest and sincerest members the elders of its church. In turn the elders of each community should appoint its humblest candidates as bishops or diocesan overseers. Finally the bishops should raise their humblest colleague to the position of patriarch or of Peter's successor. No leader should want either power or title. As at the time of the apostle's dispute, the leader who does want exclusive power or honorary titles proves thereby that he does not qualify as a leader of Christ's church. Moreover it would be well to have short-term elections and make retention in office depend on the leader's present disposition rather than on his virtues of the past. Religion must give up once and for all trying to imitate the techniques of Madison Avenue or be satisfied to be an instrument of hypocrisy. The attentive reading of the Acts of the Apostles should convince anyone of Peter's non-authoritative direction and of the democratic leadership of the early Christian church.

Immediately after the Ascension, Peter proposes to the other apostles to fill the vacancy of Judas. The decision however was made by the eleven apostles who cast the lots. Peter takes the leading role in preaching on the first Pentecost Sunday. He cured the lame man at the gate of the temple, called "the Beautiful." He preaches to the crowds who witnessed this wonder. In name of the others, he answers the accusations of the high priests Annas and Caiaphas. He unveiled the insincerity of Ananias and his wife. He cures a good number of sick brought to Jerusalem from the neighboring villages. Having been summoned a second time to appear before the religious court, he answers that his allegiance is to God rather than to men. "But when the apostles in Jerusalem heard that Samaria had received the word of God, they sent to them Peter and John." (Acts 8, 14.)

Simon the magician offered Peter money to clue him in on the apostles' secret power. Apparently he thought that driving out bad spirits and replacing them by the good spirit would be an easy way to make a living if only he knew the trick. Peter set Simon straight on his greed and contemptuous plans of using religion for the sake of making money. Peter was also the one who healed Aeneas of Lydda, who had been bed-ridden for eight years from a stroke of paralysis. Furthermore Peter brought the woman-disciple Tabitha of Joppa back to life. Still when Peter admitted the gentiles to the Christian fold by baptizing Cornelius of Caesarea, his kinsman and friend, he was at odds with his colleagues in Jerusalem. Clearly he had made a change of policy without obtaining their consent. After explaining to

117

them that he had acted upon what God had suggested in a vision, they agreed to overlook his use of jurisdiction. (Acts 11, 3.)

Later on, fanatic Jewish church leaders from Judea (Jerusalem) came to the church of Antioch with the disturbing news that circumcision and the law of Moses were still compulsory. Paul and Barnabas decided to bring this matter before the highest authorities in Jerusalem consisting of apostles and elders. Peter sided with the Antioch delegates. Then James, the honorary president of the assembly, made a motion in favor of Paul and Barnabas. The final approval however was given by the majority. (Acts 15, 1-22.)

Paul gave the council of Jerusalem a briefing on the subject matter of his preaching to the gentiles. The council consisted of James, Peter and John, the pillars of the church along with a number of other elders. "But when Cephas came to Antioch," Paul tells us, "I opposed him to his face because he stood condemned." (Gal. 2, 11.) Peter's improper attitude, publicly denounced by Paul, consisted in playing a misleading role during his visit to Antioch. The faithful of this locality were half-gentile and half-Jewish Christians. In the beginning of his visit Peter ate with the gentile Christians and paid no attention to the Jewish dietary rules or customs. Later on, when some sectarian Jews from James (Jerusalem) also arrived at Antioch, Peter suddenly avoided the gentile Christians and joined the Christians of Judaic origin. He did not want the sectarian Jerusalem leaders to know that he approved gentile Christians. Peter's conduct was creating confusion and disturbance in the Antioch community. Insincere diplomacy is unbecoming a Christian leader, and Peter found out that he did not have the final say.

And yet Peter was truly the great Christian leader whom everybody loved and admired, although not everybody always accepted his advice. Gradually Simon learned that, like everyone else, he was subject to errors, weakness and mistakes. Only an unbalanced person would think that he was any different. Peter knew that he had to watch his step and stop wanting to shine out above his colleagues. His biggest and most unforgettable mistake was that he had denied his beloved Master, as a result of wanting to be a "big shot." Having learned his lesson and as proof of the existing spirit of collegiality, he shied away from honorable titles and the use of jurisdiction. Apparently he must have refused the position of bishop or chairman of the mother church of Jerusalem. The honorary presidency was held by James the brother of Jesus who, in all probability, was not even an apostle.

Peter had learned that rank was worldly consideration and that jurisdiction was worldly power. The person who on the contrary wants to win God's favor must stay clear of all these trinkets. A good leader does not look for popularity. The words of Christ kept ringing in Simon's ears, "Whoever would be great among you must be your servant, and whoever would be first among you must be the slave of all." (Mk. 10, 42b-43.) Because Peter had made a greater effort in serving others, everybody looked up to him with the filial love which children have for the one who is a wonderful daddy, because he cares enough about finding the right answer.

Nor did Paul, the great apostle of the gentiles, dabble with power, rank or jurisdiction. He too, carried out the desires of the elders of Jerusalem, of Antioch and even of the churches which he founded, as long as their wishes did not conflict with the real needs of his beloved sheep. Such was the system of the early church, that the outstanding examples of the community became elders, and that the elders went to God for the solution of their problems. "And when they (Paul and Barnabas) had appointed elders for them (the faithful of the churches which they founded) with prayers and fasting, they (Paul and Barnabas) committed them (the faithful) to the Lord in whom they (the faithful) believed." (Acts 14, 23.) We find only one case of excommunication in the N.T., the one of the incestuous man who lived with his father's second wife. (1 Cor. 5, 1-5.) This was not an excommunication for heresy, but for bad example. Paul does not pronounce it, but warns the elders of the church of Corinth to purify their ranks.

Immediately after telling Peter, the predicted humblest servant of his church, to feed his lambs and sheep, Jesus explained to him what a top Christian leader has to expect. "Truly, truly I say to you, when you were young you girded yourself and walked where you would." Jesus is here referring to Peter's former character of following his personal inhibitions. He goes on to say, "But when you are old you will stretch out your hands and another will gird you and carry you where you do not wish to go." (Jo. 21, 18.) Jesus is now predicting Peter's crucifixion, whereby Simon would finally consent to give his life for his principles. The fourth evangelist who witnessed the fulfillment of this prediction and who wrote long after Peter's crucifixion had taken place, says that Jesus made this statement to indicate what kind of death Peter had to undergo, nl., a violent death. (Jo. 21, 19a.) Then coming back to the main point of Christian leadership which was the point Christ wished to make, he says that Jesus told Peter, "*You* follow me." In other words, never mind what happens to John or to anyone else. A good leader must be able to control himself more than others but serve others more than he serves himself.

Peter did follow in his Master's footsteps clear unto the death of the cross. He led and fed his sheep by service, example and unselfish love. The apocryphal "Acts of Peter" state that Simon chose to be crucified head-downwards, because he felt himself unworthy to be crucified in the same manner as Jesus. By his crucifixion Peter became Christ's successor and the "Good Shepherd" of the sheep for whom he gave his life. His leadership had lost its boastful coloring. By concentrating on the needs of the sheep, he became the great Christian leader. He led his sheep on to fresh water and fed them in the green pastures of unselfish love. Good leadership is beyond a doubt the hardest thing on earth to achieve, but of all human achievements, good leadership is by far the greatest feat!

As we have said, good leadership is neither an easy task nor a pleasurable thing. Should we seek authority to make ourselves important then we are not helping others but feeding our pride. If it is wielding power that we want, we are holding back on leadership by preventing our subjects from becoming mature. If it's material things that we are after, then our leadership is not serving the people but merely enriching ourselves. Christ preferred having no leaders at all to having political hirelings in directing his church. These are the leaders who boast up the structure, hoping to reap honors and promotion from their worldly-minded bosses. Ezekiel (34, 8) describes them as shepherds who fatten themselves but let their sheep go hungry. The fact that a religious leader is feared and has to be flattered proves that he has no interest in the welfare of the sheep. An institution which gives one man power over another has lost the mature Christian form of leadership and gone back to the O.T. system of force.

A person who is stuck on himself is necessarily a bad leader. Only the man who loves God and his neighbor enough to be indifferent to money, power and fame is sufficiently detached to direct a religious group. Where would one expect to find ideal leaders if not amongst those whose profession it is to talk on morality? Did not Jesus tell his leaders that they are the salt of the earth and the light of the home? Religious leaders who are not humble servants spread darkness instead of light. They feel a constant need for publicizing the little good which they really have done. Good leadership like good merchandise does not need to be publicized. Good quality speaks for itself.

Poor leadership is the major reason why society has fallen apart. History does not record any large revolutionary movements against leaders who were "good and faithful" servants. Revolutions were launched against leaders who were no good at all. Still rebellion has rarely brought about a genuine improvement. To improve a situation, the new leader must be better than the one who has been overthrown. Responsible leaders come from a society where the majority of the people are responsible citizens. That is why a society usually has that kind of leadership which it actually deserves. Whether the people elect crooks into office or do not prevent them from getting into power does not alter the situation. If we want good leaders we have to teach responsibility from the cradle on. Parents, teachers and local church leaders have to become aware of the seriousness of their job. The grass roots of lasting reform usually come from below and rarely from on top. History is one continuous story of how bad leaders have been overthrown, only to have worse ones step into their place.

The home is the place where youngsters get their basic training. The local church is the place where the family gets its advanced course. In church services the need for self-discipline should be explained. In church gatherings the right sentiments of social help should be put into practice. People are social by nature. They come

121

to church to discover the correct way of directing their love and their feelings. Unselfish love puts us in the right spirit and contributes to the good functioning of our body. Selfish love makes us feel rotten because it disturbs the correct activity of our nerves and glands. Self-interested love leads to hatred and greed, jealousy and revenge, murder and suicide. Love must therefore be purged and fed even as our food is tested by the board of health. In our final chapter we will try to examine the real meaning of Christ's words "Feed my lambs and feed my sheep."

Chapter VII

THE REFINEMENT OF LOVE
(THE LAST SUPPER OR THE FIRST MASS)

Knowing that his hour had come to depart out of this world and return to his Father, and desiring that the fire of unselfish love he had kindled would continue to glow on to the end of time, Jesus held a farewell meal with his disciples called "THE LAST SUPPER," Jo. 13, 1-2; Lk. 12, 49. "I have earnestly desired to eat this passover with you before I suffer; for I tell you I shall not eat it until it is fulfilled in the kingdom of God." (Lk. 22, 15-16.) Then, referring to the cup, Jesus says, "Truly I say to you, I shall not drink again of the fruit of the vine, until that day when I drink it new with you in my Father's kingdom." (Mt. 26, 29.)

The characteristics of this meal are that it can and will be eaten again in the heavenly kingdom. This meal is therefore a meal of love, as no earthly food can be eaten in a spiritual kingdom. Only love has its initiation here on earth and its fulfillment in the hereafter. When faith and hope will have passed away, love will still remain. (1 Cor. 13, 8 and 13.) If such be the case, the question arises whether this love meal was really a meal at all, particularly the Jewish passover meal, or was it only an independent ceremony?

The Last Supper Was a Passover Meal

All four Evangelists emphasize the fact that the last supper was a passover meal. Luke 22, 7-8 says, "Then came the day of Unleavened Bread, on which the passover lamb had to be sacrificed. So Jesus sent Peter and John, saying, 'go and prepare the passover for us, that we may eat it.' " The synoptics bring out the fact that Jesus sent his disciples "on the first day of Unleavened Bread" to make the passover preparations. With these words they are stressing the importance of unleavened bread in the passover of Jesus, more so than the exact calendar date on which it took place.

The feasts of Passover and of Unleavened Bread were taken indiscriminately. They began at 6 P.M., on the fourteenth of Nisan (April). The latter continued on for seven days. When John 18, 28 insinuates that the Passover of that year fell on Friday 6 P.M., the Jewish Sabbath, he is doubtlessly talking about the Passover according to Pharisaic custom. However, the Qumran monks and the Essenes started the new year and consequently also the eating of the Passover as early as Tuesday evening of the same week. (A. Jaubert, La Date de la Cène). Jesus no doubt celebrated his Passover at an earlier date, as did these other groups, perhaps on Wednesday after 6 P.M., the Jewish Thursday.

The New Testament ties up with the Old. If we wish to understand the new Passover, we must also be familiar with the significance and ceremonials of the old Passover. Let us jot down a few points of general interest. The Jews started their religious New Year with the feast which meant most to them. On the evening of the fourteenth of Nisan, one or more families (enough to consume a whole lamb) were to kill a one-year-old unblemished lamb or goat, and roast it. They were to eat it that same evening, together with unleavened bread and bitter herbs. In the first Passover, recorded in Exodus 12, 1-32, we read that during the Egyptian captivity, the Lord ordered his people to kill a choice lamb after sundown of the fourteenth of Nisan. They then had to sprinkle the two door posts and the lintel of their houses with its blood, and eat the flesh. At midnight while going through the streets, the Lord would PASS-OVER those houses which were sprayed by the blood of the lamb, but he would enter the homes of the Egyptians and destroy the first-born of all men and beasts. Whatever historical value these details may have is beyond the scope of our study. Their principle value is apparently a moral lesson.

Passover was the commemoration of the Jewish deliverance from Egyptian captivity. All subjugation was considered to be a punishment for past unfaithfulness to God. Because the Jews had to make a hasty flight out of Egypt, the Lord had prescribed the use of unleavened bread for seven straight days. The real point of the prescription was that leaven is a symbol of deception. Yeast blows the dough up to more than normal its size. The eating of the bread without leaven indicated the spirit of sincerity required to deserve God's deliverance and also the price which the Jews had to pay to have peace among themselves. Thus it was that, at the first Passover, the Jews became a free nation under the law of God and the direction of Moses.

A listing of the Passover ceremonials, as they were performed in Jewish homes, will give us a better idea of what the original festivity was all about.

1. The *Cup of Kiddush* was held up to the group by the head of the family or the master of ceremony, while invoking God's blessing over the Passover celebration. The father then drank the whole contents of the cup and purified himself by washing his hands.

2. *The Charoseth* dish was prepared with fruit paste and bitter herbs. It was now placed on the table with the lamb, the unleavened bread and the wine. (Offertory)

3. Before partaking of the meal, the whole family purified themselves by washing their hands.

4. The *Passa-Haggada* is the story of the Passover or the story of the liberation of the Jewish people. The head of the family was generally the narrator. He explained to his guests how their forefathers suffered under the oppression of the Egyptian captivity and how God liberated his people from the hands of their enemies. During the final Egyptian plague, God *passed over* the houses of the Jews because the Jews had acknowledged him as their God. They had carried out his instructions by sprinkling their homes with the blood of the lamb and by eating the bread without yeast. The Scriptural lesson was followed by singing a psalm (any one from 112 to 117). The psalm chosen was one of praise and thanksgiving. The Jews thanked God for having delivered them from their enemies. The whole congregation then gave its approval by taking a sip of the second cup of wine.

5. When the Scriptural reading was over, the Jews began to eat the meat of the lamb in a reclining position. The eating of the lamb was the main part of the old Passover meal. Only at Passover did the

Jews recline while eating. The relaxed position of laying at table was the sign of a free people. Normally the Jews sat at table as token of their subjection to the Romans. Because God had set them free at their first Passover, they reclined during its annual commemoration.

6. The next item was the blessing of the bread. The father thanked God for the gift of food. He then broke the unleavened loaves in small pieces. Each member took the pieces, dipped them into the common charoseth dish of bitter herbs and then ate his snack.

7. The fruit of the vine was blessed in the same manner. The father took the cup of wine (the third cup) and thanked God for his thirst-quenching gift. All present joined in his prayer of thanksgiving and took a sip of the same common cup. The Passover concludes with the longest of the psalms of praise (ps 136) called the Great Hallel.

The New Passover

With this brief outline in mind, we are in a better position to grasp the real meaning of Christ's final meal. The reader will recall, that we asked ourselves whether the last supper had anything to do with the traditional Passover meal or not. The answer to the question lies in the correct understanding of the different trends of both the Old and New Testaments. The object of the O.T. writers was not only to teach us morals but to predict the mission of the Messiah as well. In the same way the N.T. writers besides morality are deeply concerned with letting us know how the O.T. predictions were fulfilled in the person of Jesus. This is particularly true in the case of all four evangelists. Obviously the O.T.'s main object was to teach us rational human behavior often with stories which were sometimes historical, sometimes fictive or a mixture of both. The amazing thing is that some of the personalities and happenings of these stories in certain instances portray an important future event in the life and teaching of the Messiah. That is why stories of this nature have been called prophecies and their authors prophets, because they foretell future events of God's intervention or the Messiah's role.

Even the ceremonials contained in the books of Moses, such as those concerning the Passover, are symbolic and refer to some form of rational human behavior. The symbol reminds us of an inner disposition to which the Messiah wanted to draw our explicit attention. Christ did not want religion to become a meaningless mechanism and the religious-minded a group of robots. Unfortunately the Jews themselves often did not understand the purpose of their laws nor the real meaning behind their ceremonials. The reason for this lack of understanding was that they had their noses too close to the grindstone or to the scrupulous observance of the letter of the law. That is why Christ had to remove this rigidity. Blind obedience to a law, with an obsessive fear of breaking it, prevents the good spirit of love and common sense from ever seeing the daylight. The spirit of good judgment must be freed from legislative shackles. As John (3.8) puts it, "the spirit blows where it wills," meaning that the godly way of thinking adapts itself to human needs as to degree and importance. Consequently we should not be looking for a strict order of rituals in the account of the last supper which we find at the traditional Passover celebration. Here the application of the meaning behind the rituals is the thing that counts.

1. THE TOAST. In the Jewish Passover the head of the family opened the ceremonial meal with the "cup of Kiddush." He drank the whole contents of the cup and then continued to wash his hands. Even to this day, to drink to something is to go along wholeheartedly with a person and his projects. By drinking the first cup and by purifying himself before the others, the father expressed the condition of good leadership. A good leader must be the first to set the right kind of example. Moreover, the father was also uniting himself with the sincerity and sufferings of his forefathers. We may not forget that these were the virtues by which the ancient Hebrews earned their God-given freedom.

At the last supper, Jesus does not have to unite himself in thought with the ceremonial of sacrificing a lamb or with the sufferings of exemplary predecessors. He himself *is* the symbolical lamb of the first Passover, the innocent Isaac whom his Father was willing to give up to teach people not to do their own will but God's will instead. He is "the Suffering Servant" ready to be slaughtered. Suffering violence and persecution is his way of life, his cup of tea or, as the N.T. calls it, "the Cup of the Lord." Moreover, if the Hebraic expression of "giving one's blood" means giving one's life, then Jesus can justifiably propose his way of life to his followers by saying, "Take ye and drink the cup of suffering, as I drank it during my whole life and am about to drink it in its entirety. Soon I will give my blood or my life to draw you away from the captivity of irrational sense-indulgence." Instead of standing up and fighting for his rights, Jesus chose to part with his possessions and, if need be, his life. Willingness to suffer injustice instead of defending his titles has become his way of overcoming violence and greed. Surely Jesus did not have to drink a toast to be reminded of his forefathers' willingness to endure sufferings. The cup of Kiddush was the story of his life. He could truthfully say, "THIS CUP IS ME!"

2. THE OFFERING. The next ceremonial was putting the food on the table. The essential items are the charoseth dish, the lamb the unleavened bread and the wine. This ceremony requires no particular explanation. It is self-evident that some sort of gift is necessary for the performance of religious services and for the support of church ministers. Jesus said that "the laborer deserves hi wages." (Lk. 10, 7.) The only difference between the offerings of the two systems is that the O.T. prescribed the gifts which were to b offered at a religious service, while Jesus left the size and nature o the gifts up to the generosity of the giver.

3. PURITY BEFORE COMMUNION. When the table was se and dinner served, everyone had to purify himself by washing hi own hands. The meaning behind this ceremony is of vital importanc at the Lord's Supper, where love has to be purified of its irration; elements. "Whoever therefore eats the bread (of sincerity) or drink the cup of the Lord in an unworthy manner," says Paul, "will t guilty of profaning the body and blood of the Lord . . . and (he) ea and drinks judgment upon himself." (1 Cor. 11, 27-29.) Jesus speal in similar language about Judas Iscariot. This apostle fell so low th he handed his best friend over to his executioners for the sake money. Using his Master's trust and the knowledge of his wher

128

abouts he set Jesus up to be disposed of by his enemies. After his traitorous deal with the top religious schemers, he had the guts to sit down at table with Jesus and partake of his food. As Jesus remarks laconically, "It would have been better for that man if he had not been born." (Mt. 26, 24.)

It just so happened that Judas betrayed Jesus, the head of a figurative body, of which the followers are only the members. (Col. 1, 18; 1 Cor. 6-15.) Had Judas not betrayed Jesus but only a member of Christ's body, his guilt would have been equally great. This story is written as a warning to all Christians not to go back on the essence of their promise. Judas' betrayal is not merely a recording of an historical event. Like all parts of Scripture this story was meant to teach us a lesson. John tells us that "Anyone who hates his brother is a murderer and . . . no murderer has eternal life in him." (1 Jo. 3, 15.) A follower of Jesus has made a solemn commitment to love and to forgive. If he breaks his promise by nourishing ill-feelings, he is as guilty as a pagan who murders his enemy. The worst injustice a heathen can do is to take another man's life. The worst thing a Christian can do is to break the solemn pledge of the thing that makes him a Christian.

There is consequently more than one way of making one's self totally unworthy of participating in a meal of love. Hatred and betrayal are as bad in a Christian as murder is bad in a man who has no faith at all. Judas is only the symbol of those who have betrayed their friends in Jesus. By heaving a deep sigh of disturbance and then making the statement "Truly, truly I say to you, one of you will betray me" (Jo. 13, 21), Jesus forces everyone to examine his conscience. Although conscience is a matter between the individual and God, yet most of us are inclined to find excuses for ourselves. That is why every one of the disciples asks Jesus to be the judge of whether he is guilty "Is it I, Lord?" We learn from this story that we need the help of others to form a correct opinion of ourself.

Outside of betraying friends to the extent of Judas, there are other less serious ways of destroying exceptional confidence. Granted that minor weaknesses do not constitute a formal breach among friends, they nevertheless prevent that kind of closeness which Jesus wanted his followers to have. Luke 22, 24-27, places at this point the rivalry of the disciples for power and for glory. Which one of them would have the right to tell the others what to do? Power, jealousy and ambition are the forerunners of the betrayal of friendship. They eventually turn love into sentiments of hatred and distrust.

Coming back to the dispute of the disciples, the fourth Evangelist tells us how Jesus dealt with the situation. Without saying a word, he got up from the table and girded himself with a towel. Then pouring water into a basin, he began to wash the feet of his disciples. Just how cheap the apostles felt by this gesture is brought out by the vehemence of Peter's protestation: Jo. 13, 4-11. The conclusion need hardly be spelled out. A Christian leader must not rely on power, but on humility, service and love. If the Master did not boss his own subjects but became their servant, who are they, as equals, to be pushing each other around?

Fear of public opinion is another form of moral weakness, which easily breaks up Christian closeness. We find it in persons whose goal is to get ahead in the world. When people set their hearts on things they lose their principles. Fear of displeasing the worldly minded who can rob us of our possessions and inflict physical harm is undoubtedly a very powerful argument. Just recently Jesus had asked the sons of Zebedee if they were able to drink the cup of sufferings which he as a sincere person was compelled to drink. (Mt. 20, 22.) When they replied affirmatively, it was evident that they were not fully aware of the difficulty of keeping such a promise. Genuine friendship knows no limits when a friend is in real trouble. A friend in need is a friend in deed. Jesus now warns his disciples, Peter in particular, of the fact that when in danger, they would cease to be a friend. Again the fourth Evangelist has placed this episode where it belongs, nl., during the examination of conscience at the meal of love. (13, 37-38.) Everyone is supposed to examine the sincerity of his own feelings and the quality of his spirit of sacrifice. A non-imaginary love of God depends on the sincerity of our love for people. (Mt. 5, 23-24.) This genuine altruistic love is the condition of the new covenant between God and man, just as the external observance of the rules of purification constituted the terms of the old covenant. The drinking of the cup, as we will soon see, is merely an outward pledge.

4. LOVE'S FAREWELL SPEECH. After the wound has been cleansed it must be treated with the right kind of ointment. An instruction on God's readiness to forgive, restores hope to a person who has lost confidence on account of his guilt. The Passa Haggada was the story of God's mercy towards the Jewish people. The farewell discourse of the last supper is the story of God's love towards all peoples, in particular the followers of Jesus. Those who remain united to Christ's principles, as the branches are united to the vine, will obtain the glory of their leader. The importance of these stories, which later developed into a reading and explanation of the Scriptures, is brought out by the amount of time given to them in both the old and the new Passovers. In them we should find the special thought for holding a commemorative service of the Lord's supper. Every religious leader should carefully prepare the particular message which he intends to give for the occasion.

At the Last Supper Jesus begins by explaining why he had a strong desire to eat this Passover with his disciples. "Having loved his own who were in this world, he loved them to the end." (Jo. 13, 1b.) His love for his followers had prompted him to institute a regular service wherein the main points of Christ's final meeting would be passed in review. The new Passover would not merely be a reminder of the courage exhibited by their ancestors. Instead, it would be a personal examination of how well they were able to turn the cheek. Like a father on his death bed, with his loved ones all around him, Jesus tells his followers that he is returning to his own heavenly Father. One last favor is what he asks of them, namely, that they be good to one another as he was always good to them. Mutual love is his final word, his last recommendation, his NEW COMMANDMENT. Replace selfish interest by mutual dedication. (Jo. 13, 31-35.)

He goes on to say that they should not be saddened on account of his departure, because he is only going to prepare a place for them in the mansions of his Father. They will soon follow him to these mansions, for now they know the way. The unselfish way that Jesus lived and accepted sufferings is the only way that leads to God. It makes us feel for the real needs of people and direct love without doing anybody any harm. Much as Christ had to suffer from the attacks of unscrupulous people, at least he was able to live with himself. His way of living is the only road that leads to happiness. "I am the way, the truth, and the light." (Jo. 14, 1-7.) While saying these things Jesus did not raise his voice. He spoke in a soft and confidential tone. His disciples, Peter, Thomas, Philip and Judas, not yet used to his figurative language, were able to interrupt him and ask him for further explanation.

As Jesus' way of living leads to the Father, so also Jesus' way of thinking coincides with that of the Father. That is why one can say, seeing Jesus is like seeing the Father. God's unselfish love is visible in everything he does. Jesus is never looking for what is more honorable, comfortable or pleasurable for himself. On the contrary he is forever looking for what is best for others. As he frequently reminds us, "I seek not my own will, but the will of him who sent me." (Jo. 5, 30b.) Unfaltering faith in the objectives of Jesus will empower the disciples to do the same wonderful things which Jesus did and even more of them. Whatever his followers ask the Father in Christ's name, meaning to bring them closer to God, that petition will always be granted. One such example amongst many is where Peter prayed that the man born lame and begging at the gate of the temple might obtain the use of his legs.

On condition that the disciples live and love by Christ's standards, Jesus will ask the Father to send them his spirit of truth and understanding to help them solve their problems. The worldly-minded will not have the light of truth to guide them, because they are living by the wrong set of principles. Jesus will not manifest his way of life to them. They will be like orphans with no one to care. On the contrary, the friends of Jesus will be guided by God's objective way of seeing human needs in their right perspective. They will have their finger on the correct heartbeat of all human needs.

Besides the guidance of the Holy Spirit, Jesus' followers will have peace of mind and happiness of heart. The same strength and consolation which the Father gave to Jesus in Gethsemane and on Calvary will carry them through their worst ordeals. No earthly motive could have sustained Jesus during his own trial and execution. The peace and comfort of his Father is what kept him from going out of his mind. Truly this peace is a peace which the world cannot give. It was given to Jesus at a time when no earthly motives were able to sustain him.

During his life Jesus had all the fears and pains which every one of us would have had under similar circumstances. The only difference between us and him was that he never was interested in material gain or personal success. What kept him from giving up or having a nervous breakdown was his astonishing faith in God. His marvelous success could lead us to think that he was one with the Father not only in thought but also in strength. His power to overcome difficulties would then have been easy for himself but hard for us. To prevent us from ceasing to see in him a monument of strength and endurance, he reminds us by saying, "My Father is greater than I." The strength and peace which Jesus received from his Father will be the legacy to his followers in times of distress. If the prince of this world or the powers of evil were incapable of upsetting the spirit of Jesus, neither will they be successful in disturbing our own peace of mind. (Jo. Ch. 14.)

These same thoughts are further developed in Chapters 15 and 16 of John, where Jesus talks about the vine and the branches, spells out the bitter persecutions which await his followers and amplifies on the assistance of God's spirit. The life of his followers here on earth may be as painful as the period of a woman in labor. Yet, as these pains prepare for the birth of a new child, so their suffering will prepare for unending joys which will be permanently theirs.

Chapter 17 of John is the closing prayer. In it Jesus asks his Father to give him the glorious reward which was planned for him from all eternity, because he has established God's kingdom on earth. "Father, glorify me in your presence with the glory I had with you before the world was made." (Jo. 17, 5.) He then prays that he might be recognized by all men as God's emissary. The proof that Christ was God's emissary lies in the fact that "no one ever spoke like him," no one ever lived like him, no one ever loved like him and no one ever died like him. Then follows the most beautiful prayer which was ever composed. In this prayer he asks all his followers to be as closely united to each other as he is one with the Father. This unity between Christians and Christian groups is the only sure proof to outsiders that Christianity is the right kind of religion and not merely a form of fanaticism and hypocrisy. Truly the story of how God loved the Jewish people and sent Moses to liberate them from Egyptian captivity can hardly compare with the story of how God loved all people and sent Jesus to liberate humanity from the enslaving effects of irrational love.

5. THE ASSIMILATION OF THE SPIRIT OF THE LAMB. We have now reached the height of the old Passover meal which consisted in the eating of the lamb. Although Jesus did eat of the lamb, the lamb's consumption had turned into a meaningless celebration. That is why the Gospels only vaguely allude to it with the words, "And as they were eating." . . . Mk. 14, 22; Mt. 26, 26. In reality Jesus was the one symbolized by the lamb. It would be senseless for Him to unite himself in thought with himself. Not only was the figurative lamb a superfluous symbol where the real lamb had made his appearance, but it would have been an invitation to cannibalism if Christ, the real lamb had intended the words "take and eat, this is my body" to be taken in the literal sense. Consequently it was not in the literal sense that Jesus' body was to be eaten nor was it in a literal sense that his blood was to be drunk. These words obviously have to be taken in the *only possible* alternative meaning which is a figure of speech. The spirit of Jesus' sincerity is what we are told to eat and the spirit of Jesus' willingness to suffer is what we are told to drink. These two qualities of complete unselfish living were Christ's way of life, or, as the Orientals put it, "this is my blood" meaning this is my way of life. Communion with the spirit of the lamb is therefore the thing that is assimilated in the new Passover.

Just as the role of the prophets, including the Baptist, had ceased with the coming of the Messiah (Mt. 11, 13), so also the custom of slaughtering and eating the passover lamb had lost its meaning when the real lamb was sacrificed once and for all. The slaughtering of the animals was only the symbol of our irrational love and

134

pleasures which actually should be sacrificed. Self-indulgence is the ultimate cause of all social disturbance and of the disturbance of peace and freedom. The cruel death which the innocent Son had to undergo at the hands of sinners is a much stronger deterrent of sin then the slaughter of animals. "When the perfect comes the imperfect will pass away." (1 Cor. 13, 10.)

6. THE NEW PASSOVER MEAL OR THE EATING OF UN-LEAVENED BREAD. Apart from its pragmatic suitability on a hasty journey, the eating of unleavened bread had definitely a very special meaning. The Lord had told the Jews to eat this bread during their speedy escape into Egypt. The real meaning of unleavened bread, however, consists in the fact that it is made without yeast or leaven. *Leaven was the symbol of corruption and insincerity.* Eating unleavened bread signified one's intention of being sincere to God and also to everyone we meet. Saint Paul tells the Corinthians, "Throw out the old leaven (of insincerity) that you may become a new dough." (1 Cor. 5, 7-8.)

With this meaning in mind Jesus blessed the symbolic bread, which means he thanked his Father for the food of truth and sincerity. In the old Passover the Jews thanked God for the bread which feeds the body. Here Jesus thanks his Father for the heavenly bread which feeds the mind. In a previous discussion, Jesus had told the Jews that God had fed their forefathers in the desert with manna which fell from heaven. The manna like all bodily food did not preserve their forefathers from death and corruption. All died even though they had eaten an abundance of the manna. Now God sends his Son from heaven to feed our mind the eternal food of truth. If we assimilate Christ's spirit of sincerity, we not only feed the right food to our mind but we will preserve both body and soul onto a glorious resurrection.

Sometimes our offspring resembles us like two peas in a pod. Besides physical resemblance there can be moral characteristics as well. Christ uses a similar image. "Unless you eat my flesh and drink my blood you shall have no life in you" is therefore the equivalent of saying "unless you assimilate my principles and live by my standards, God will not save or reward you." (Jo. 6, 26-58.)

Whether love be sincere, rational, unselfish or altruistic it all means the same thing. Such love comes from God and leads to heaven. Unless we believe in the hereafter, we will never fully know the value of this precious gem. Faith in God stimulates the growth of unselfish love. Love without faith will never be totally unselfish. God is therefore the author of unselfish love, because without faith in God or without taking Jesus' manner of living into the boat of our life, our love will always go back to personal interest. We can therefore truthfully say that charity or unselfish love is God's gift and of such incomparable value that we can never sufficiently express our gratitude for having received it. The Greek word *eucharizesthai* means to bless or to give thanks. That is why besides being called the Lord's Supper, the Last Supper was also given the name of the Eucharist. In this meal Christ thanked his Father for the food of sincerity and the right kind of human love.

When the thanksgiving prayer had been said, Jesus presents the bread of sincerity to his disciples and tells them to take it and eat it. By eating this bread, we solemnly pledge sincerity and friendship to each other as members of Christ's body. After describing the Last Supper scene, Saint Paul lists the different spiritual functions in the early church. He then compares them with the members of our own body. Though each member has a different function, they are all supposed to cooperate harmoniously with one another. He concludes by saying, *"You (Christians of Corinth) are the body of Christ and individually members of it."* (1 Cor. 12, 27.) The conclusion of St. Paul's early writing is not hard to understand. By eating the bread of sincerity, we solemnly pledge sincerity to one another. Our promise of fidelity makes us members of Christ's body or as Jesus said, "This is my body." Should we, however, eat this bread unworthily, i.e., without the intentions of levelling with people, we eat and drink judgment onto ourselves, just as Judas did.

7. THE DRINKING OF "THE CUP OF THE LORD." The final important item of the Passover is the drinking of the third cup of wine. In the old Passover the drinking of the cup was preceded by a prayer of thanksgiving. The Jews thanked God for the fruit of the vine, the drink which slakes the thirst of the body. In the new

136

Passover, Jesus blesses "the cup of the Lord." He thanks his Father for the drink of unselfish love which slakes the thirst of the soul. We all thirst for love but we do not all love in such a way that we quench our thirst for love. Unselfish love alone can satisfy the human thirst because such love alone is rational or unselfish. Unfortunately, unselfish love cannot be had without self-restraint and endurance of injustice. This complete libation of one's self, as Saint Paul puts it, is the mysterious meaning of "the cup of the Lord."

The faithful followers of Jesus must drink the bitter contents of this cup, because no one can have principles without having to pay the price of defending them. Sticking to the principles of sound judgment and taking the rap that goes with holding a firm stand are the conditions of obtaining a glorious resurrection. By sticking to his guns and suffering for the cause of justice, Christ entered into the glory of his Father. God had reserved this glory for him and for his followers when he decided upon the constitution of the world. Though Christ's human nature abhorred the bitter contents of this cup in the garden of Gethsemane, yet he consented to drink it. "Oh my Father, if it be possible, let this cup pass away from me; nevertheless not as I will but as thou wilt." (Mt. 26, 39.)

This same cup Jesus now presents to his followers with the words, "Take it and drink it." Again the meaning is easy to understand. If we accept to drink the Lord's cup, we promise to turn our cheek to injustice and live a life of self-abnegation. Just as this cup signifies Christ's willingness to shed his blood in order that sinners might stop sinning, in the same way our drinking of the cup implies our willingness to suffer persecution for the sake of justice.

Surely the Last Supper has eminently carried out the moral lessons typified by the ceremonials of the old Passover. The "agapai" or love feasts which preceded the Lord's supper in primitive times of Christianity, being as it were a remnant of the old Passover, soon fell by the wayside. *Though the breaking of ordinary bread with our fellowmen* is the application of the principles of charity, it is not a food of the mind but a food of the body. The breaking of unleavened bread with the Lord is a spiritual meal. An intense spiritual meal, such as the Lord's Supper, can hardly go hand in hand with the filling of one's stomach. When the apostles returned with food from the city of Sychar, they presented it to Jesus and said: "Master, eat." Having given the Samaritan woman the bread of sincerity and the living water of unselfish love, Christ's mind was not set on feeding his body. The two do not really mix. Jesus therefore refused to take the bodily nutrition and told his disciples, "I have meat to eat that you know not." (Jo. 4, 31-32.)

In like manner, the observance of the Lord's supper, though occasionally tied onto the synagogue reunions of the Sabbath for reasons of conversion, was from the beginning of Christianity preferably placed on "the first day of the week." "The first day of the week" had become a current expression. (Mk. 16, 2.) It was Christ's V-day and was known as "the Lord's day." (Rev. 1, 10.) On that day, Christ rose from the dead and gained a decisive victory over his enemies and their use of violence. Christ had lost the battle but he had won the war! No law prescribing the people to commemorate the Last Supper on Sundays was originally imposed. Jesus had abolished man-made laws in favor of rational direction. He replaced church-legalism with the mature individual's freedom of choice. (Rom. 14, 5-6.) On account of the complete trust and extreme closeness which existed among the Christians, "the saints," as they were called, did not need a threat to get them to come together. They held their eucharistic meals as often as they possibly could and preferably on Sunday in order to purify their love of the elements of our common weakness.

IN RETROSPECT

We have now come to the end of our study on the philosophy of Jesus, which is at the same time a study on the nature of love. Surprisingly enough, we have not found any significant discrepancies between the philosophy of rational human behavior, the philosophy of Jesus or the teaching of the Bible. All three systems have taken into consideration the well-established psychological findings on human behavior and on the functioning of the mind and the will. What they have added to these findings is that man does not go through life like a drifter in a boat, without having sails or rudder to guide him. Man is able to determine his course. His will may be hampered by personal limitations and the influence of his environment, but unless he is mentally deficient, he can either pull himself together or glide along with the stream. His love for people is either all-inclusive or he runs into the misfortune of being stuck on himself.

Love is real when it is genuinely concerned with the existing needs of people and when it renders help in a sensible way. Love is beneficial when it stimulates the health of mind and body. Love is good when it puts our conscience at ease and treats others as equals. Love is lasting when it produces no harmful effects. Love can be biogenic as the rays of the sun or necrotic as the chemical gases of warfare. It all depends on how it is directed.

We have considered the essential aspects of human love: What it is and how it is meant to be used; its power of influencing others; how to preach unselfish love without causing resentment; how to undo the harmful effects of past irrational love; a few outstanding examples of those who succeeded; how to lead a group of people intent on having the right kind of love; how to refine love to prevent it from becoming destructive again. What more can be said on the subject of love or religion?

We all know that it is impossible to live without love. The reason why people have guilt feelings and stir up trouble is usually because they are unable or unwilling to control their affections. When we help where no help is needed or do not help where people are in distress, then our feelings are sick. Satisfying people's erratic desires or closing our eyes to the needs of others is failing to comply with the demands of reason. When we abandon our rational principles, we lose the right to freedom and to be treated with respect. Rationality is contact with reality. Contact with the real is putting the other person's real needs on the same level as our own. It implies a great deal of self-control. It means taking care of other peoples' needs as if they were our own. Most people pretend to be interested in others, when they are only interested in themselves. While chasing after colorful butterflies or reaching for an edelweiss, they fall over a cliff or break a leg. When in serious trouble we all remember the words of Cardinal Wolsey to his companion in prison, "Oh Cromwell, Cromwell, had I but served my God with half the zeal I served my King, he would not, at my age, have left me naked to my enemies." (Shakespeare—*Henry VIII*.)

When it is too late, people realize that it would have been much easier to suffer a little injustice than to suffer the consequences of their own mistakes. Voluntary acceptance of injustice has made heroes and martyrs, because it has taught people the need to forgive. Refusal to accept injustice has made communists and rebels, because it has taught people to hold on to their rancor. No one can lead a good life without accepting a certain amount of injustice. It is up to everyone to decide if the cause for which he is suffering is deserving and if he's capable of taking it with a smile.

Students are up in arms against the insincerity of their leaders. They resent the constant interference of society in private affairs. While the older generation respects good and bad leaders alike, the newer generation loathes those who fail to make the distinction. The older ones do everything to please. The younger ones do everything to displease. The older connive and produce. The younger complain and leech on. Failing to go along with the rational demands of society is just as wrong as failing to disagree with the irrational ways of poor leaders. Both extremes lead to tension and to violence. All extremes whether right or left are a distortion of the superlative power of love. It is because everyone naturally sets his heart on fantasies and on dreams, that Jesus taught us a love which sticks to the Real!